WINDS of PROMISE

BODIE & BROCK THOENE

THOMAS NELSON PUBLISHERS
Nashville • Atlanta • London • Vancouver

For my brother-in-law, Howard Turner,
a man of the greatest personal integrity,
and one of those unique individuals
who can be relied on at all times.

PROLOGUE

The thin man was covered in trail dust. His knee-high boots were innocent of any polish. His slouch hat was as shapeless as a flour sack. The prospector's cheekbones were highlighted with patchy whiskers, emphasizing instead of concealing his youth.

Walking with a jaunty step, whistling "Mairin-ni-Cullinan," the miner hiked down the trail toward the river. Though the Gaelic words were "All the winds are blowing gusty, with a storm of tears," he was smiling.

He wore a small pack on his back, containing a single spare shirt and little else. But the obviously heavy padlocked crate that he carried gave notice of fortunes changed. Prospector he had been, living on bacon and beans, but that was all over now.

The rattle and jingle of harness from behind made him make way for an approaching wagon. When the empty freight rig and four-up team drew abreast, it did not pass. Instead the driver drew rein and hailed him.

"Goin' down are you then?" the reinsman inquired.

Up and down referred to the river; every forty-niner understood the usage. "Would you care for a ride?"

The walker considered. He was wary of strangers, but it was a hot day, the box was awkward and cumbersome, and the offer to let his feet rest was tempting. The young prospector shaded his eyes against the glare of the California sun and studied the features of a man much like himself in age and build. "Do I hear the lilt of the old country in your speech?" he inquired with a smile as he climbed aboard the tall-sided wagon. He stowed the crate in the bed just behind the seat.

The teamster clucked to the mules and explained that he was bound to the steamboat landing to pick up a cargo of tools for the mines. He was glad of the company on the journey. "Mayhap you'll be interested in the shipment," he said. "Since the steamers came to the river, the price of shovels has dropped from twenty dollars to five. It's still highway robbery, but better than before."

The miner shook his head. "Thanks be to the Almighty, I'm through with spadework. I have a fine wife waiting to hear the word: No more grubbing in the dirt for me."

"Aye," the teamster agreed. "So it is with me. I broke my back over many an empty pan before giving up and taking the job hauling freight. Will you be looking for work yourself?"

"I'm minded to open a business of my own."

"With your wife?"

"As soon as she joins me from the States," the

prospector announced. "I have not seen her in ten long months. And she's all I have in the world."

The two rode in silence for a time, but two Irishmen will not remain in that condition long. Their conversation ranged from the newly arrived companies of Chinese laborers working mining claims to the lack of decent food in the Sierra.

"But hold there," interrupted the ribbon handler. "The steamer has glorious grub. Oysters as would grace a rich man's table and beefsteaks big as the platter. They say a man can eat all the way from Sacramento City to the Frisco Bay. But," the teamster glanced sideways at his companion, "the passage is still thirty dollars. A princely sum, and perhaps too dear to save a bit of walking."

"I can afford that," the miner announced abruptly. Then he deflated slightly. "But there is my business to think of. I should save my poke and not fritter it away on extravagances."

The driver thought a moment and then said, "The captain owes me a favor. What say I tell him we're cousins? If I could get you half fare, would ye take it?"

"The steamer," the miner mused. "A meal fit for a king and floating all the way to Frisco." He reached a sudden decision. "I'll do it," he said. Then, because he was feeling expansive and in no mood to be closefisted, he added, "And because of your hospitality in giving me this lift and arranging the passage, what say you come along? Half fare and I pay for both, for the comradeship of it."

The teamster was caught off guard and did not know

what to say for a moment. "I cannot," he said. "My duty lies with the cargo."

"A pity," the miner said. "Then I'll not take the boat either. If I cannot share my good fortune, I'll just save my money."

The drover snapped his fingers, making the mules prick their ears. "Why not?" he said. "I deserve a little celebration. Shovels will be as much in demand in two days as in one. We'll revel all the way to Frisco!"

The night was dark and draped in fog. The churn of the paddle wheels disturbed a heron stalking frogs in the tules. It launched itself into the sky with a loud croaking bleat.

A moment later the steam whistle of the side-wheeler bellowed a challenge to the river. The pilot used the echo bouncing off the banks of the delta to judge the bend in the channel.

Inside the steamer all was light and activity. Eating was popular but took second place to drinking. The bartender on board knew how to prepare twenty different kinds of flips, juleps, and toddies. The passengers were determined to try one of each.

Games of chance were in full swing: faro, fan-tan, monte. Many miners, fresh out of the hills and eager to carouse, would arrive in San Francisco with an aching head and an empty wallet.

A hatchway just forward of the starboard wheel guard opened, and the young Irish miner emerged into the cool air. He was still clutching the heavy crate. He checked the locks on the chest for the third time in as many minutes. Gambling held no attraction for him. What he had collected was not a sum to be blown in a night. It was a fortune; a whole new life. "Friend," he called out for the teamster. "It's a mite close in there. I'm glad you suggested coming out here for a smoke. Did you get the cigars?" There was no immediate reply.

Something in the mist-shrouded night made the miner feel uneasy and he turned to reenter the cabin. As he pivoted, he found his path blocked by a big man in a leather coat.

The only warning of attack was the leather-clad man's sudden movement. No moonlight flashed off the blade of the bowie knife that the assailant yanked from his belt.

The prospector hesitated a fraction of a second—to defend himself he would have to drop the chest. It was a fraction of a second too much delay. The point of the knife was thrust savagely upward, under the miner's ribs. The force of the blow raised him up on his toes and then he did drop the strongbox. He screamed, but another blast of the fog whistle covered the sound.

The attacker lifted the young miner on the point of the blade and by his belt; then pitched him over the rail. In a second he was sucked under the paddle wheel and ground into the depths of the river.

CHAPTER 1

The heart of the *New World* throbbed softly beneath my feet. Moored fast to the Long Island dock, the deck of the steamer trembled with the beat of her pulsing engine.

One day previous I would have said that she was quivering with excitement. Shining white for all of her two-hundred-foot length from jackstaff to stern rail, the *New World* was newly slid down the ways and ready to be discovered. Travelers from Albany to Manhattan were waiting to line the Hudson with praise for the pride of William Brown's river fleet.

Today's developments seemed likely to set a new course. *New World*'s shudders still reached the soles of my feet, but the deck tremors felt now like her death throes.

As first officer of the side-wheeler, I stood my watch in the pilothouse and was not present at the meeting place in the texas, or officers' room, just aft of me. My absence did not mean that I could not hear what was happening though. The hammering of owner Brown's fist on the mahogany table made the needle of the barometer quiver in its brass case over my head. His words threatened, scolded, and condemned his opponents to eternal darkness, all apparently to no avail.

Just after eight bells that morning, a grim-faced William Brown had marched aboard his ship, and from that instant I knew something was dead wrong. He had been accompanied by a pair of sour-faced goons whose shoulders were too big for their coats: deputies on the city payroll. Behind these crushers came men whose bellies were too big for their coats: bankers. Last of all came a man about whom the only thing that was big was his ambition: Sidney Jackson, Brown's partner.

Captain Wakeman and I were making a last inspection in preparation for *New World*'s maiden sail. Wakeman saw the bleak cavalcade approach the ship and muttered, "Trouble, I'll be bound! Trust Jackson to jam the rudder even now! Rafer," he said to me, "ring down for forty pounds of steam, and have Olson standing by. And Rafer," the captain urged, "whatever happens, don't leave your post." Wakeman met the arriving troupe on the main deck, while I communicated his order to the engineer far below.

It says something about Sidney Jackson that both the captain and I instantly assumed the man was behind whatever was wrong. As Brown's partner in the building of *New World*, Jackson whined and argued against every half-dime Brown spent. Had Jackson had his way, *New World* would have been an underpowered, stripped-down cattle boat instead of the glorious floating palace that she was.

But here is the shank of the business, as I gathered from Brown's shouts: "What matter that we were three days late launching? You know that we pushed the yard to work miracles as it was. Why even that three days was only because my partner" (I could hear the sneer on Brown's face without seeing it) "changed my order to use only American iron in the boiler tubes. His penny-pinching would have blown the *World* to kingdom come if I had not caught it and corrected it."

Here one of the portly financial swabs must have interjected something, for when Brown spoke again he was shrill. "Show me where it says that." And then, "But what is the point? Because your thieving paper says you can steal my ship, can you run it?"

Whatever answer he received must have been the coal oil in the furnace because there was a tremendous crash against the aft bulkhead and the sound of smashing glass. Other voices shouted in chorus with Brown's and then all the cries dissolved into the noise of a brawl. I moved toward the hatch, remembered Wakeman's strict order, and returned to grasp the spokes of the wheel.

The clatter of the donnybrook quieted at last, and then Wakeman and one of the dour guards joined me in the wheelhouse. "They've done it," Wakeman said, paying no more mind to the guard than if the man were a clot of washed up seaweed. "They've stolen her. Jackson approved a clause that let the bank foreclose on the loan if she was late a-launching. Three days," he added bitterly.

"But why? Doesn't Jackson lose by it too?" The second hired watchman, every bit as talkative as the first, joined his comrade in sullen silence. Their scowling faces looked as if they would welcome a chance to cool us out.

Wakeman shook his sandy-colored hair. "Not a single copper cent! Didn't you hear the hubbub? That was when Brown discovered the bankers had cooked a deal to sell *New World* to Jackson. Brown used up all his money in seeing her fitted out proper, and then Jackson comes along and steals her!"

I knew Brown's temper. "But surely Mister Brown won't let the matter stand!"

His eyes brightening at last, Wakeman reported, "Mister Brown got some of his own back—Jackson will be eating only soup or porridge for a time." Then he frowned again. "But it seems that may have been part of the plan too. Take a look." He hooked a thumb over his shoulder toward the dockside. There I saw Mister Brown being marched away toward a Black Maria police van and that scum Jackson holding his jaw and being helped into a carriage. "By the time Brown is free from the assault charge, the bankers and their pettyfogging lawyers will have *New World* fast in their clutches."

"But what can we do about it?"

At this point the first side of beef dressed as a deputy sheriff proved that he was animated after all by speaking. "Nothing! You don't do nothing but shut her down, see? Me an' Finn are here so that nothing happens to Mister

Jackson's property." The thug removed a canvas sack of slungshot from his coat pocket and flipped it with menace into his meaty palm.

To my surprise Wakeman agreed. "Right. Mister Maddox," he said to me, "make preparation for shutting her down. Signal the engineer to tighten the relief valve."

I started at his unexpected words. "But, captain—"

"Just do it, Mister Maddox," Wakeman ordered gruffly. "And be quick about it. Just because you don't relish what's happening does not give you the right to disobey an order."

I saw it clearly in an instant. The captain's words were intended to lull the sheepdogs to sleep while we made ready to bolt! "Aye, sir," I agreed, relaying the order to the engineer.

The soft *sooh, hah, sooh, hah* of the engine continued its steady beat as belowdecks the closing of the relief valve allowed the steam pressure to build. "Why don't the engine stop?" Finn demanded. He was a bright one too, he was.

"Now you know that we must clear the boilers," Wakeman replied smoothly. "If we leave standing water in the tubes then it will rust the condenser, sure as you're born."

Finn nodded knowingly. "Don't do nothing to hurt this boat," he warned. "Right, Liam?" The other gorilla nodded and pursed his lips to show the concern he gave his duty.

"Ring up for fifty-six pounds," Wakeman ordered me. "And have Olson stand by to hook up."

What was concealed beneath the captain's calm phrasing was the command to build the pressure to the point where it would power the giant cylinder and to be ready to engage the paddle wheels. Wakeman casually stepped beside Finn and inspected a thermometer. As he studied the mercury-filled tube, he idly grasped the brass-bound handle of the steam whistle and coiled a couple feet of rope in his hands.

"I see squalls ahead," the captain observed to nobody in particular.

"Where?" Finn demanded, leaning out to look at the clear blue sky.

"Here," Wakeman retorted, spinning the wooden whistle pull at the end of the slack and cracking Finn sharply behind the ear. The guard slumped with a groan.

At that instant I barreled into Liam and bore him to the ground. His great, bearlike grasp played havoc with my ribs, but before the wind was altogether crushed out of me, Captain Wakeman borrowed Finn's blackjack and sweetly tapped Liam on the temple as well.

"Well done, Mister Maddox," Wakeman said. "Tell Mister Olson 'up bar,' if you please." He yanked downward on the steam whistle till *New World* screamed as if he were twisting her tail. Then he hacked off the length of rope with his jackknife and tossed it to me. "Tie him up with that," he said, nudging the unconscious Finn with his boot toe. "And find something suitable for his friend." Then out to the railing he went, hollering to the deckhands, "Let go aft! Let go forward!"

By the time I returned from the texas a moment later,

the great buckets of the wheels had begun to revolve. Slowly at first, and then picking up speed, *New World* reversed away from the slip. As the ship gathered way, Wakeman took time to study my handiwork with the second thug. "Did you have to use a sash cord, Mister Maddox? Velvet is too good for the likes of him!"

We were standing up in the middle of the channel before Finn shook his head and looked at us through pain-crossed eyes. "You . . . ," he muttered. "You can't do this. We're depadys."

"Deputies are supposed to prevent theft, not assist in it," Wakeman observed. "And I suggest you keep a civil tongue in your head or you'll swim home."

The captain called down through the speaking tube for Olson to idle the boat and to join us in the pilot-house. He ordered all the crew to assemble there as well. When we were gathered, he explained what had just taken place and then detailed his plans. "We are leaving this ungrateful harbor and going where *New World* will get the respect she deserves. I'll put any of you ashore who do not wish to join us."

"Where are we bound, Captain?" I asked. "New Orleans?"

"Too crowded," Wakeman said. "We're headed where *New World* will be the queen of the river—the goldfields of California. Ho for San Francisco Bay, men! What do you say?"

To a man, we all agreed to stay with the ship.

We set the two deputies off in the captain's gig.

As we said good-bye to the States, we saw them

rowing back toward the shore. Or rather Liam was rowing. Finn held one hand to the back of his head, while he
shook his other fist at *New World*'s stern.

Once we cleared the harbor and shaped our course
southward, the reality of what we were undertaking set
in. It was our intent to take *New World*, designed and
built as a river steamer, on a journey of eighteen thousand miles. In all my twenty-eight years, which included
ten before the mast and the last five on the river, I had
never heard tell of the like. Leaving in mid-April as we
were, we bid fair to reach the Horn in the dead of the
Southern Hemisphere's winter. What was more, being no
doubt pursued by Jackson, and having no ship's papers,
we were likely to run afoul of some authority or other on
the trip.

Since the *World* only drew five feet of water, she was
not designed for rough seas. This fact, together with our
constant need to refuel her, meant that we would have to
hug coastlines and sail in the lee of islands whenever possible. Being unable to take to the wide ocean increased
both the length of the voyage and our risk of running
into a less than cooperative administrator.

Nevertheless, Captain Wakeman was sanguine about
our chances. "She's solid, Rafer, and built for speed. We
can turn fifteen knots. We'll double the Horn and be at
the diggings before you know it."

We coasted down the eastern seaboard, putting in at

Savannah to coal up before striking across to Havana. I do not know what fancy talk Wakeman used on the Georgians, but no one seemed to notice our lack of official documents. When we made landfall in Cuba, Wakeman gave the crew shore leave, crossed the palms of the Spanishers with some of his own gold, and soon we were provisioned and under way again.

The skipper was brave, but he was no fool. We steered clear of British ports, knowing them to be sticklers for proper clearances. Wakeman told me privately that the English were not above seizing improperly registered vessels and hanging such as us for piracy. By feeding *New World*'s hungry fires on a mixture of coal, bought from complacent Dutchmen, and ironwood, chopped by us on lonely cays, we contrived to cross the Caribbean unmolested. Not without alarms, I might add; coaling at St. Maarten, for example.

New World burned a cord of wood an hour or about a ton of coal a day. The bunkers aft of the boiler room could not hold fuel for more than two days' travel. To ease us past uncertain ports, Wakeman contracted for twenty tons to be stowed in the main salon. The crystal chandeliers had already been crated and stored, but he had us cover the parquet floors and the wainscotted walls with sailcloth.

It was not rigging this improvised storage that waylaid us though. Wakeman had failed to inquire as to the loading dock facility in St. Maarten. Anyway, when time came to coal up, here came a parade of native women dressed all in scarlet or crimson or bright orange. Each carried a basket on her head, and—that was how the fuel was loaded: twenty tons deposited in the salon, one hatful at a time.

Anyway, as Wakeman sweated and shouted, to which he got polite, smiling nods in reply, the time for our dawn departure slipped away. It was noon before the last of the women trudged back up the gangplank for the last time.

No sooner had we cleared the harbor than Wakeman sighted a smudge of smoke on the horizon. Clapping the glass to his eye, he announced that she was an American gunboat. We all held our breath for some minutes, until the captain finally sighed and allowed that she had entered the harbor and was not in pursuit of us.

We were off Recife when Gutterson, one of our deck-hands, gave a shout from the jury-rigged crow's nest hanging from the stack. "Sail, ho!"

"Where away?" I returned.

"Coming up astern!" was the reply. "I see three masts. She's running with all her canvas set and . . . Mister Maddox! She's turning toward us!"

Wakeman must have heard the ruckus from inside his cabin. He flung open the pilothouse hatch, seized a telescope from the rack, and an instant later was tromping on the wheelhouse roof over my head. His voice floated down to me. "Mister Maddox! Ready to come hard to starboard and make a run for the coast. Three masts could be a clipper—or a warship."

That the unknown vessel was steering directly for us was soon apparent to all our crew. The knife-edge of a black bow was pointed straight at us. My hands were tense on the spokes of the wheel, ready to spin the helm and race for shelter in shallow water where a warship could not follow. Then Captain Wakeman's relieved voice sang out, "I can see her masthead pennant; she's an American trader."

At that news we all relaxed. Minutes later, the clipper ship drew up on our port beam and the skipper backed his sails. The narrow deck was jammed with all manner of men: some that looked like farmers, others lawyers, still more clerks; a whole shipload of gold fever victims. "What ship and where bound?" Wakeman called.

"Clipper *Rainbow*, fifteen days out of New York and bound for San Francisco. You?"

"The *New World*," Wakeman said proudly. "Also out of New York and San Francisco–bound."

The other captain tipped his hat back on his head. "I have heard," he shouted through his speaking trumpet, "of a steamer by the name *New World* that was stolen in New York. What a coincidence."

"Isn't it?" Wakeman replied smoothly.

"A stolen vessel would have to look sharp south of here," the clipper's captain continued. "I hear there's a British ship of the line cruising below Rio."

"If we sight the stolen vessel I'll mention it to her captain," Wakeman replied. "I'm sure he'll be grateful for the word."

With that the clipper put up her helm, reset her sails, and bore away from us to the southwest, dwindling to a speck on the horizon.

Before she was even out of sight, I was already discussing our situation with the captain. "How can we expect to stay clear of everybody who wants to hang us for another fifteen thousand miles?"

Shrugging, Wakeman answered, "Nothing to be done but keep on course. I'll study on it some, Rafer. Meanwhile, you take us to Rio." Then he showed what he was really reflecting on. "Curse the luck! Why didn't I think to take on passengers? Did you see Rainbow's deck? Two hundred emigrants at $150 each, or I'm a mudsucker! Thirty thousand dollars!"

Two days later I was again at the helm and Gutterson again manning the lookout. Just before I sent him aloft he had come to me to ask if he could be excused the duty. He said he was not feeling well, and truth-to-tell, his color was not good. Gutterson was nicknamed "Nuck" for the way he knuckled his brow to anyone smarter than himself. By his own cheerful admission, this category included almost everyone. Good-hearted and amiable, he was no sailor, though he tried hard. Barely adequate as a deckhand on river duty, he had been frequently seasick since New York. Today his befuddlement seemed greater than usual. I was minded to send him below, but Wakeman countermanded me, saying we had six men down ill already and could spare no one from their assignment.

An uneventful hour passed, and then I heard a thud

on the pilothouse roof as if we had been struck by a meteor. When my shout to Gutterson brought no response, I called a man to take my place while I climbed the ladder aft of the texas to see what was amiss.

Nuck Gutterson was sprawled on top of the wheelhouse where he had fallen from the stack. He was feverish and his complexion was the color of egg yolks. As I carried him below, he vomited black bile and cried out.

Stretching him on the bench at the rear of the wheelhouse, I went in search of Wakeman. When I found him he was not surprised at my news.

"It's the yellow fever," he concluded. "The men who have it—seven now, counting Gutterson—must have gotten it in Cuba."

"Is it contagious?"

The captain shook his head. "No, the rest of us are in no danger—but there is nothing much to do for these poor devils either."

At night, in the pitch black off of Rio de Janeiro, we committed the bodies of three men to the deep. When I urged Captain Wakeman to seek medical help in Rio for the four survivors, he scowled and cursed at me. "Do you want us to lie up in quarantine and rot? Stow the sick ones in the forward hold and keep them quiet! That's an order!"

For a day and a night I sweated in the close confines of the forward hold—a dark, airless place with only four feet of space between decks to accommodate my near six-foot height. Down the constricted throats of the fevered men I spooned water into which I had mixed the juice of limes. There was nothing else to be done; there was no cure for yellow fever.

Wakeman sold off some of the furnishings from the main salon and bribed the customs officials to be perfunctory about their inspection. Then he provisioned us with fuel and supplies. We got under way again at dawn of the second day, with the sick spread across the foredeck to catch the fresh breeze.

Three more of them died. Only Gutterson, delirious and raving or sullen and silent by turns, survived.

The deaths left us shorthanded, but there was no remedy for it. If we tried to ship replacements and any hint got out of the fever, we would be either quarantined or barred from every port in South America.

CHAPTER 2

We were south of Brazil and steaming toward Montevideo when the oft discussed British brig crossed our course. She turned toward us and hoisted a signal ordering us to "heave to and prepare to be boarded."

Captain Wakeman was of no mind to comply. If we could reach the harbor at the mouth of the Rio de la Plata, the British would have no authority to molest us. As the skipper himself was at the helm, he ordered me below to explain matters to Engineer Olson.

Down from the weather deck I ran, dropping through the gangways past the social hall and main deck three rungs at a time. In the engine room I found Olson, calmly ordering the "black gang," as the stokers were called, to heap the furnace with more coal while he studied the steam pressure gauge.

"Captain needs more speed," I said. "British warship wants to board us."

Olson nodded and passed a bandanna across his sweaty, bald dome. "Are they upwind or down?"

"Down. They'll have to tack to come up on us."

The engineer nodded again. "Bring me an oar from the captain's launch."

Despite the strangeness of the request, this was no time to argue.

"Now, sonny," Olson continued when I returned with the oar (he talked that way to everyone except the captain), "don't ever let me catch you doing this." With that admonition, he took the paddle and wedged it between a bulkhead and the top of the steam relief valve, jamming the safety valve shut. "That ought to give us another three knots, sonny," he said. "Tell Cap'n not to push her for more'n twenty minutes though, or we'll be flying over Montevideo 'stead of sailing in."

If I had arrived in the engine room at high speed, I matched or exceeded the pace getting back topside and as far from the boiler as possible. The British ship fired a round from her bow chaser, but the shot fell astern of us and Wakeman laughed. "We've got the advantage of her," he said.

Just then there was another puff of smoke from the small cannon and a shot whistled into the aft main deck and splintered a lifeboat. "She's got the range!" I yelled.

"Not for long," Wakeman said through gritted teeth.

Another shot missed, then another crashed into the texas and ripped a hole in the wall of my cabin before splashing into the sea. "Ten minutes gone! If they hit a paddle wheel we're finished," I observed.

"They won't."

The next shell started a fire in the crew quarters aft.

I went to see to it, found the blaze already extinguished, and dashed back to the wheelhouse.

Eighteen minutes had passed. I reminded Wakeman of Olson's warning. "Just another five hundred yards," the captain grunted. "We'll be inside the shoals."

I was so engrossed in keeping track of the time and the cannon fire from the warship that I had not even noticed where Wakeman piloted us. Green water foamed on all sides as the ship hurtled between two exposed pinnacles of rock. "Twenty minutes mark," I said. Wakeman gave no sign of having heard.

The next three shots from the warship fell astern and it was at last apparent that we were winning the race. The brig upped its helm, away from the shoal water, and put back out to sea. At twenty-three minutes by my Rockford pocket watch, Wakeman signaled the engine room to relieve the pressure and resume normal speed. "We won that one," he commented, patting the helm with affection. Then he added, "But the British have reason to dog us now. They'll be waiting outside the harbor for our exit."

When we dropped anchor off Montevideo, Wakeman was again smiling, but he did not share the cause of his good humor. "Mister Maddox," he said. "Pick two oarsmen and accompany me in the launch."

I could not imagine how he had resolved the difficulty so easily. To have no papers meant no escaping seizure by the British and that would mean the end of our voyage.

We were nearing the customs dock when the captain

stood up suddenly in the bow of the rowboat. He waved to a tan uniformed soldier standing on the pier, shouted something in Spanish by way of a greeting, and promptly fell into the bay.

Sputtering and floundering, Wakeman splashed more than necessary for a man whom I knew to be a good swimmer. The men and I quickly pulled him out, but not before a large crowd of soldiers and other onlookers had gathered on the dock. I shot Wakeman a look full of question, but he only grinned slyly and shook his head. It made me wonder if he was coming down with the fever after all and was off his head some way.

When we landed at the customs pier, Wakeman shook the drips from his curly hair and turned his pockets out until he stood in a puddle of seawater three feet across. He patted his dark blue officer's coat and his face took on a look of horror. In frantic-sounding Spanish he accosted the customs official and demanded to be taken to the American consul, *muy pronto*.

At once, the official agreed. Was the American captain quite all right? If the sailors would remain at customs, the captain and his first officer would be conducted to the United States consulate right away.

His feet squishing inside his boots, Wakeman led a little cavalcade across the market square to a squat whitewashed building flying the Stars and Stripes. Once there he plunged inside, startling an astonished secretary and getting immediate access to the consul's inner office.

"Mister Bloom," Wakeman addressed the consul. "I'm Captain Wakeman of the steamer *New World*. I have had an accident in the harbor while coming ashore; nearly drowned. Barely got out alive."

"Gad, sir," Bloom said sympathetically, looking at the captain's soggy clothes and disheveled hair and beard. "Sit down, sit down. Here, have some brandy."

Wakeman accepted with thanks, then with a rueful expression on his face said, "What's worse, I fear our voyage to California will end here."

The consul was instantly solicitous. "Why? What do you mean?"

"I was advised by the captain of the clipper *Rainbow* to be certain that our sailing manifest was in order, as some British warship was accosting American ships on the high seas and demanding to examine their papers. I was on my way here to ask you to verify that all was in order when I fell into the bay . . . and my papers were lost!"

Bloom actually laughed. "Is that all? Tut, man, don't lose heart so easily. I can vouch for you; better yet, I'll draw up new papers for you right now and I'll sign them myself. Here, Keppler!" he shouted to his secretary. "Take Captain Wakeman's mate and draw up a bill of particulars about the ownership, mastery, and destination of the American steamer *New World*. And be quick about it."

It was clear from the way he leaned on the word *American* that Consul Bloom was in a bellicose mood; he would not let American honor be trampled by pushy Britishers. In fact, he said as much, hooking a long, boney thumb over his shoulder at a daguerreotype of

President Zachary Taylor, the hero of the Mexican War. "Old Rough and Ready there would not let American sovereignty be questioned, and neither will I. Give Keppler the particulars and we'll do the rest. Call back in an hour, gentlemen; all will be ready. Oh, and here, take this five-dollar gold piece to purchase clothes and food. Travelers' aid to fellow Americans in distress, you see. And if there is anything else to be done for your assistance here in Uruguay, don't fail to call on me."

Wakeman was still laughing when he was dressed in dry shirt and trousers and the two of us were eating and drinking in the plaza. "New papers, new clothes," he chuckled, "and grub to boot, courtesy of the United States. This is rich." Wakeman shook his head at a peddler displaying bright red sashes and ignored a comely señorita who hung over his shoulder.

"What will happen when Bloom finds out that he has assisted a piracy?"

Wakeman waved a dismissive hand. "Don't give it a thought. We're shoving off soon and will be long gone before he hears about our little difficulty back in New York."

"I meant, what will happen to him?"

"You are a queer duck, aren't you Maddox?" Wakeman said with a smirk. "Haven't you learned by now that looking out for yourself is the only concern in life? A queer duck."

Though addressed to me, his last comment was overheard by another serape-clad peddler, pressing forward with wickerwork cages of tropical birds. "Not ducks, señor," the vendor corrected, "parrots. They can learn to speak."

"Just the ticket," Wakeman said, tossing a handful of pesos at the man. "I'll have that one, there." He pointed to a scrawny, blue and yellow parrot with bedraggled feathers and black lines like tattooing on the bare skin of its face. The bird screeched when its cage was passed to Wakeman, then croaked and whistled at the dark-haired señorita. Its eyes flashed at the pretty girl as if pleading to be rescued from the captain.

"What do you want it for?" I asked.

"I'll teach it to say 'queer duck' to remind me what a soft heart my first officer has," Wakeman said.

Wakeman soon tired of his joke and would have pitched the parrot overboard had I not asked to have him. Because of the lines on the bird's face, I named him Scrimshaw. The tracing of black feathers reminded me of the ink drawings whalers did on sperm whale teeth and the like.

By crumbling bits of sea biscuit between my fingers and speaking softly, it was not long before Scrimshaw was perching on my arm and eating out of my hand. The bird did well enough on hardtack, but I soon discovered that he had an unexpected affinity for other foods as well.

Standing my watch during the nights made for lonely passages, especially as we traveled farther and farther down the long tail of the South American continent. I took to carrying Scrimshaw's cage into the pilothouse with me, and would sometimes let him out to perch on the bench back of me. I would speak to him, winning his confidence and helping to pass the time.

On one particular evening, Nuck Gutterson joined Scrimshaw and me. The deckhand was off watch and should have been in his bunk below, but since his recovery from the yellow fever, he had not been able to do enough for me. He scrounged the galley (taking his life in his hands if he had been caught by Elijah, the cook) to bring me a two-in-the-morning bracer. Gutterson unpacked a canvas stuff sack by the light of the lantern over the chart table.

"I couldn't find nothing 'cept crackers and a tin of sardines," Gutterson apologized. "I dasn't light a lamp, on accounta 'Lijah would feed me to the sharks!"

"Never mind, Nuck," I said. "You didn't need to bring me anything. I'm just glad for the company. And Scrimshaw likes crackers."

The blue and yellow bird was already happily munching his ration, which he grasped with one claw. At the noise of Gutterson's jackknife sawing into the lid of the sardine can, the bird's head popped upright and he intently studied what the crewman was doing. Just as Gutterson speared one of the oily fish, Scrimshaw flapped over and snatched the sardine off the knife point.

"Give that back!" Gutterson scolded, waving his arms in protest.

"Wait," I urged. "Let's see what he does with it."

To my surprise, the parrot plucked a bit of the preserved herring with his curved black beak. The light of the lamp flame reflected in his eye, which pulsated with interest. "Hello," he said distinctly, with exactly my tone and inflection. "Hello, hello, hello."

Our passage round Cape Horn was one of charting a fine line in our distance from the deserted, rock-bound shoreline. Too close in left us no room to recover should we lose the engine; too far off put us into the teeth of the gale.

Staten Land, which we coasted past for hours at fifty-five degrees south latitude, was surely the most desolate place on earth. It was a frozen, craggy landscape of perpetual snow. No one lived there, nor could they, there being nothing to burn for heat or use to build shelter. In the long watches, with the seas constantly changing direction, I was mindful of how awful it would be to become castaway on such a bleak shore. Life would not long persist.

It came to me that at home the blossoms of the apple trees had given way to swelling buds, but here all that bloomed were ice crystals. My breath froze on the glass of the pilothouse windows, making it nearly impossible to see out. Spray breaking over the bow so coated the jackstaff and the foredeck that it resembled a frozen pine tree standing atop a skating rink.

The watch aloft was reduced to thirty minutes per

man, and even then men came down with frozen cheeks and frostbitten noses. Scrimshaw huddled inside his wicker cage, with a blanket tucked up close around it and the whole affair close beneath the lamp for warmth. He still shivered and I fancied his "hello" was deeper and more hoarse than before.

As if coping with the ice and the freakish currents were not enough, this southernmost tip of the Americas was prone to unexpected blows that come out of a clear sky. In fact, just as currents in water are difficult to detect unless they carry some floating object along in their stream, so it was with the winds around the Cape. We were making good progress, having finally left Staten Land in our wake, when we spotted a brig some two miles to the north of us. Her sails hung limply in a flat calm and her nationality could not be deciphered because the flag at her stern drooped so slack.

Suddenly, without warning, a blast of air shook the sailing ship like the grip of an unseen fist. Her jib was torn free of its rigging and flapped itself to rags in less time than it takes to tell.

The torrential breeze struck the *New World*. She heeled over to port, then righted herself as Scrimshaw's cage bounced to the floor and broke open. He screamed a protest, flying up to my shoulder to perch. Both of us hunched our heads down between our shoulders to keep warm.

The wind ceased as suddenly as it came. In the calm, a light snow began to fall. I was steering by compass, mainly, with reference to a pair of rocky pinnacles on the starboard bow called the Puerto de Muertos, the Gate of the Dead. How apt the old Spaniards were when it came to names.

Queen Calafia's fairyland, for instance. California was reputed to be a land of warmth and sunshine and incredible riches. It was said that since the first discovery in '48, gold could be found there as plentiful as the snowflakes drifting down outside the wheelhouse. Men with simple tools like picks and shovels and handmade sluices were made fabulously wealthy by a hundred feet of streambed. And it was all there for the taking: no one to object, no thieving wretches like Sidney Jackson to interfere with a man's hard work.

I saw it very clearly: a warm, summer day beside a gently bubbling spring. A single shovelful of loose earth turned into a rocker. When I bent over to look, a dozen gleaming nuggets, each bigger than my thumb, winked up at me. A beautiful woman, twirling a parasol, strolled over to join me.

Struck dumb by her beauty, I could not speak. Mutely I selected the largest gold nugget and offered it to her. She smiled and the glow of her smile warmed me down to my toes.

She leaned toward me. I felt her long, dark hair brush my cheek. Her lips pressed against my ear. And then, she bit me!

I came awake with a start and knocked Scrimshaw across the wheelhouse. "What did you . . . ?" I shouted. Then I stared out into the storm. Where were the rocks? Where was the Gate of Death? Frantically scanning the horizon, I spotted my landmark—on the wrong side of the ship! As I dozed, the subtle current pushed *New World* aside until we were headed straight for the shoals!

Spinning the wheel till the spokes seemed to disappear, I cramped it hard to port as far as it would go and held it there. Rocks were everywhere in front of me; jagged teeth ready to tear out the bottom of the ship.

With agonizing slowness, *New World* at last responded to the helm. Crablike she walked sideways away from the danger. An ice-topped dagger of stone reached out for the starboard paddle wheel, grazing the housing. I leaned away from the danger, as if my puny force could make the boat turn harder, quicker.

A gap appeared between foaming breakers and *New World* straightened up on her course. A minute later she was out of danger. Only then did I notice that a chunk of my earlobe was gone and blood dripped from my cheek to my shoulder to the floor.

I picked Scrimshaw up from the corner where he had fallen. My blow had broken a few of his tail feathers, but caused no other damage.

Staunching my wound with a pocket handkerchief, I soothed the bird, thanking him for being the instrument of a merciful Providence. When my watch was relieved, I said nothing in reply to Wakeman's gibes about the injury. Instead I took Scrimshaw to my cabin and we shared a tin of sardines.

CHAPTER 3

After what seemed like months in the frozen grasp of Cape Horn, we finally crossed some invisible line and escaped. We turned northward into the Pacific, warmer waters, and the second half of our journey to San Francisco Bay.

New World put into Valparaiso. We expected to stay longer than our usual restocking forays because the men needed time ashore. Also, Olson and his gang needed time to repair the ravages of the constant buffeting of the Cape passage.

Valparaiso, the Valley of Paradise, was halfway along Chile's rocky coastline. It was home to a good harbor, luxurious haciendas built by wealthy padrones on the heights above the bay, and earthquakes. The waterfront was also home to obnoxious smells. Chile was justly famous for its leather, but the smell of the tanning works made me anxious to put back to sea.

While in port, the captain and I met up with John Simm, master of the brig *George Shaddock* of Boston. She was homeward-bound, having left California some forty-five days earlier. But it was not Simm's tales of fortunes found and lost in the goldfields that intrigued us; it was far more personal than that.

The *Shaddock* had called at Panama City on her way home. Aside from hordes of goldseekers anxious to obtain passage north, Simm had also encountered a pair of deputies and one Sidney Jackson willing to pay for information regarding the whereabouts of *New World*. How they had tumbled to our destination, I do not know, but since we could not hope to avoid refueling in Panama, they were waiting there in ambush.

"Why tell us this?" I asked. "Now that you've seen us, why not reverse your course and collect the reward yourself?"

Simm looked as if I had struck him in the face. "I took the time to hear the straight of the matter from others out of New York," said he. "Some would chart the matter just as you say, but not me. I know Jackson and his kind; grasping devilfish that he is! I like to think that if it were me trying to avoid his clutches, others would warn me."

"And what do you suggest?" Wakeman wanted to know.

Simm frowned unhappily. "Besides the two goons who follow Jackson like a pair of misshapen shadows, he has hired some armed guards to back his play. What with his writ for your arrest and the seizure of the ship, I don't think bribing the port officials will serve your turn."

"You didn't answer the question," Wakeman persisted.

Shaking his head, Simm said, "There is nothing for it

but to give up your plan of going north. Why don't you put about and go back to Montevideo? You could spend a year on that coast and then try again; maybe Jackson will give up and go home."

Wakeman and I looked at each other in consternation. "We did not round the Horn and come this far to turn the *World* into a coal barge or timber freighter," Wakeman said doubtfully. "Still, Jackson has got the cork in the bottle."

It was my turn to show some sand, and my idea came out without time to reflect. "You're right; we've come too far," I said. "What say we put into hiding near Panama City and I'll go ashore and reconnoiter? You would be recognized at once," I pointed out, "but not me. Let me go size things up before we turn tail and run."

Wakeman seized on the idea, but Simm warned, "You are risking more than you know. At best you are certain to be arrested and hauled home to stand a charge of piracy. More likely Jackson's thugs will squeeze what they want from you and then you'll be crocodile bait. Don't do it."

But Captain Wakeman's mind was already made up, and I was too proud to draw back. Three days later we steamed out of Valparaiso on course toward the north and a likely noose around my neck.

East of the port of Panama City there was an island just offshore called Tabago. Located near the mouth of the

Rio Chepo, Tabago was small, overgrown with tropical vines, and fit for little except to breed snakes and diseases. No one lived there but a few poor fishermen who supplemented their meager incomes with smuggling.

The shelter provided by the lee of the island created a small anchorage for the native craft. There was also just space enough for *New World* to tuck herself in out of sight of the shipping lanes.

I rigged out in gear from the slop chest, exchanging my dark blue uniform coat for a thin linen jacket. I shaved off my imperial and knotted a yellow silk cravat up close under my chin. My slicked-back hair was the color of buckwheat honey. I looked quite the dandy.

"Do your scouting quickly and get back," Wakeman advised. "I don't trust the natives overmuch. For us to be hanging here without contraband to sell confuses them. But as soon as the confusion wears off they will soon figure out how to sell our whereabouts to someone."

Leaving Scrimshaw in the keeping of Nuck Gutterson, I climbed into a dugout canoe, passed a handful of silver to the paddlers, and set off for Panama City. As they rowed I had time to reflect on the oddity of the place. Scarce fifty miles due north of where I floated on the waters of the Pacific was the Atlantic that we had left months before. Scrimshaw could have flown from one ocean to the other in a couple hours, while *New World* had carried me thousands of miles to get there.

Panama City was built by the Spanish conquerors back in the 1500s as a base from which to attack the South American tribes in Peru. The English privateer

Henry Morgan sacked and burned the place, but the Spaniards rebuilt it before losing it to Colombian revolutionaries. Since then, Panama City had been mostly ignored, or deliberately avoided as a mosquito-infested sink of sickness. Until the California gold rush, that is.

Panama City got new life as a way station on the route to the diggings. In order to speed up the journey and avoid the rigors of a Horn passage, miners from the States would take ship in New York. Then they would put in at Chagres on the Caribbean side, cross the Isthmus by mule and canoe, and then in Panama City would obtain seagoing transport for California. There was even talk of a railroad across the Isthmus to hurry the travelers along.

Despite the California trade, Panama City looked dangerously decrepit. As much flaking plaster was heaped at the bases of the walls as remained on the crumbling adobe. Only the twin towers of the cathedral hanging over the town gave any hint that this city would not disappear into mud at the next rainy season.

My oarsmen brought me to a beach below a stone wharf. The market space had once been a grandly roofed arcade. It was now open to the elements and only a few crumbling pillars remained of the covering. The dockside was crowded with native women wearing white dresses hawking everything from bananas, mangoes, and red peppers to cheapjack trinkets and pet monkeys. Raggedly clad fishermen displayed sole, barracuda, and squid; and a whole herd of brown-skinned children, wearing little else than skin, begged for pennies.

The next thing that caught my eye when I got ashore were the notices: every piling, adobe wall, and closed shutter was papered with images of the *New World*. The handbills were headed with a very good likeness of the side-wheeler just below the word REWARD in three-inch-high letters. The posters proclaimed the ship had been stolen in New York. Information leading to her recovery and capture of the pirates would be worth three hundred dollars. There was also a description of Wakeman, but not one of me. I plucked a copy from the wall of the Gato Negro cantina then sauntered inside to see what scuttlebutt I could gather.

The proprietor, a dapper mestizo, offered me *agua ardiente*. "Drinking the water here is *peligroso*, señor," he said. "Better you drink the spirits." I thanked him for the counsel, but opted instead for a plate of chicken and rice.

The other patrons were mostly Americans. They yelled at the owner, as if to offer in sheer volume of English a substitute for their complete lack of Spanish. Despite their ill temper, the landlord kept his own good humor, refilling glasses and plates, and doing a booming trade at two Yankee dollars a meal.

A few arguments of no consequence erupted and subsided, while I scanned the crowd to see if any looked both sober and trustworthy enough to question. The goldseekers were all loud, arrogant, profane, and unruly. It was as if they abandoned their manners when they left the States.

The attention of the room was diverted from drinking

and gambling to the arrival of a group of soldiers. Though barefoot, the six newcomers all wore matching brown trousers and white shirts and carried antiquated flintlock muskets that may have arrived with Pizarro.

They roughly shouldered up to the bar, pushed through the other drinkers, and demanded to be served. There were blasphemous oaths from the Americans, but in the face of the firearms, there was grumbling assent to move aside.

When the landlord returned to my corner, I raised an eyebrow and nodded toward the soldiers. After first looking to see if he was being watched he bent toward my shoulder and whispered, "Hired guards, señor. *Hombres muy malo.* The government does not pay them much, so they hire out to whoever will keep them in coin to buy drink." Then he hurried away, as if he had already said too much.

Huddled below the bar at the far end of the room was a thin youth in obvious distress. Though a slouch hat was pulled low over his face, I could see the stretch of pale skin over gaunt cheekbones that proclaimed near starvation. The boy, no more than sixteen, hugged his thin knees and stared at nothing.

On a sudden impulse, I reached into my pocket and tossed the hungry boy a coin. I think it was a medio or fip, worth six cents.

The boy grabbed eagerly for the money, only to have his hand stomped by one of the soldiers. Another of the brutish guards pounced on the money and waved it triumphantly.

Very deliberately I stood up, crossed to the youth, and placed a silver dollar in his hand. His look of gratitude struck me hard. It seemed to say that he had received no kindness from anyone for a long time.

When I turned round again I was facing a ring of soldiers. A short, swarthy fellow with a machete thrust through a sash around his middle seemed to be their leader. He ordered the landlord to translate for him. The chief bully said that begging was not permitted and that either the dollar would be confiscated or the boy arrested.

I shook my head. This negative motion in the face of the six armed figures surprised them. Then the leader muttered something to his comrades and placed his hand on the hilt of the machete.

There was no time to waste. I hooked my arm around a steaming plate of rice on the countertop and dashed it into his face. The soldier stumbled back, rice clinging to his straggly hair and gumming his eyelids.

Hooking my toe under a small, three-legged stool, I flipped it up into my hand. When I cracked it down sharply on the counter, I was left with a serviceable club about eighteen inches long.

The soldiers were shucking their weapons off rope slings and it would have gone badly for me if the other annoyed patrons had not jumped in. Instead of my being assaulted by six at once, the room dissolved into a half dozen combats and the guns were wrenched away before any could be discharged.

My opponent's machete was in his hand and he

swung wildly, hacking a chunk out of the bar where my right arm had been before I leaped aside. I batted the blade downward with my club, hoping to knock it out of his hand, but he spun and chopped the air around him, then advanced toward me again.

Deliberately I backed up until stopped by the counter and put a startled look on my face as if suddenly feeling trapped. My attacker got a wild look of triumph in his eye, and swung the rusty blade toward my head.

At the last second I jumped toward him, catching the descending machete on the stool leg and driving him back with my rush. My left fist swung up from my waist, striking him in the throat and making him gag and choke.

Clamping my hands around his wrist, I determined to win possession of the blade. Then there was a volley of gunfire outside the cantina and a voice demanded, "Finn! Liam! Make them stop this at once! I don't pay for brawling in saloons!" It was Sidney Jackson.

Spotting an exit behind the counter, I turned to vault over the bar and escape. At the last second, and I do not know what force prompted me, I scooped up the frail boy, tossed him over the counter, and then hurdled it myself.

I suppose I did not want the boy to remain behind in the clutches of the soldiers. It was a certainty that, if left behind, he would be the target of their sergeant's revenge.

Dashing through a blanket that served as a curtain, I dragged the boy after me. I shouldered aside a cook sprinkling peppers into a pot of beans and we made our escape into an alley behind the cantina and down to the wharf. We hid behind the acres of laundry drying there and I cautioned the boy to keep still while I looked for pursuers. There was no need for the warning. My charge was mute with terror and trembling so violently that his teeth chattered. I cuffed him hard on his boney shoulder. "Do you understand English, boy?"

His mouth opened and closed then he replied with a nod. At least he was not deaf, but the little beggar was as worthless as an adolescent tomcat on a garbage heap.

"Pull yourself together!" I snapped. "Wipe that cowardly look off your face or we'll be spotted!" Another cuff and his eyes filled with tears. "None of that or I'll leave you behind!"

Clutching my sleeve pitifully, he wiped his brimming eyes with the back of his hand. I figured I had picked up a half-wit. Owing to the apparent dimness of his mind, I softened toward him although his cowardice went against my grain.

I grabbed his arm and jerked him to his feet. "Alright then. Get your legs under you. Follow me!" He obeyed, sticking close on my heels. We melted into the crowd on the dock.

In the harbor was the three-masted ship *Mosconome*. She was just setting her sails in preparation for departing. Her decks were thickly covered with passengers bound for California. Dozens more hung from her rigging and lined the rails. Her master was explaining to hundreds more on shore that he could not accept even one more.

"She'll flounder," he said with a shrug. "Don't you plug-uglies get my drift? There's no more room. You'll have to take another ship, or wait for my next trip."

"When will that be?" a tall, thin man in knee-high boots demanded. "I been here close on three weeks already. Somebody else is stealin' my gold right now!"

"The New York agent who sold me my ticket promised there would be a ship waiting here," a young Yankee asserted.

"Agent be dashed!" the captain said.

An angry murmur went through the crowd, even as *Mosconome*'s skipper was spreading his hands to say nothing could be done. The mob pressed in on him, and he looked suddenly frightened. He jumped down into his launch and shouted for his crew to pull for the ship.

A few rocks were thrown toward him, but they splashed harmlessly into the bay. The crowd, continuing to grumble, dispersed slowly, with many angry looks toward the ship.

Suddenly I knew that I had an answer to *New World*'s problem. The boy, who remained silent, stood by my side. "If you want a meal," I said, "come along. You can come back here tomorrow and be all right, I think." He readily agreed, and the native canoe rowed us back to Tabago.

Once out of sight of Panama City's harbor, I relaxed enough to study my new acquaintance as we faced each other in the center of the dugout. I had been wrong about his age. On closer inspection he seemed even younger than I had first thought; thirteen perhaps, with no sign of a beard and still a piping Irish treble for a voice.

"What's your name and how did you come to be begging in a saloon in Panama?"

"My name is James O'Reilly." He was Irish by the sound of his accent and bore the lean and hungry look of those who had come out of the great famine. Freckles stood out on his pale skin. Wisps of curly, light red locks peaked out beneath the brim of his hat. "I'm on my way to California."

"Alone?" I queried. "Where are your parents or the rest of your family? You cannot mean to go it by yourself."

O'Reilly talked with his green eyes darting all around. He looked at the shining Pacific water, at the muscled back of the paddler in the front of the canoe, and at his own, grimy, broken-nailed fingers, but never at me directly. Whether this was due to shyness, fear of strangers, or because he was about to tell a whopper, only the rest of his speech would determine.

"I'm old enough," he protested, pulling the slouch hat down forcefully as if to emphasize a quality of manly self-reliance. "I'm eighteen."

Rudeness had never been my style, but I fear I laughed aloud at the patent untruth. To say more would be to call the boy a liar and perhaps drive him into silence, so I apologized and urged him to go on. As he spoke I reassessed my first impression of him. He might have been cowardly by nature but he was no imbecile.

"I have an older brother already in California," he continued. "He went out in '49. He wrote me and asked that I join him to help work the claim."

"And your parents approve?"

O'Reilly's eyes darted toward my face, then plunged overboard again like a boated fish jumping back into the sea. "They . . . they are dead. I have no relation except my brother."

"What's his name?"

There was a fragment of a pause as if revealing the brother's name might prove risky. "John," the youth said at last.

"And can you find him easily? Does he know you are coming?"

We swung past the head of Tabago and entered the bay behind it. "He's up the river, where all the claims are."

"Which? American, Yuba, Mokelumne?" There was a stoney silence. "I don't know what you are afraid of, but let it go. Tell me how you came to be stranded in Panama."

"The agent who booked my passage down on the *Columbus* told me it was good all the way to California!"

"And you believed him? You didn't check? There is no line that operates all the way, unless you sail around the Horn."

O'Reilly's voice sounded even more quavery. "I know

that now!" The boy was again on the verge of tears. Even the lead paddler turned at the sound of the emotion-choked words until I gestured angrily for him to mind his own business. "I still would have been all right," O'Reilly continued. "But when I started out from Chagres I was beaten and robbed of all my cash."

"And you have been begging ever since?" I probed gently.

"You saw the harbor," O'Reilly said bitterly. "Captains are even turning down paying passengers. Nobody has time for a penniless tramp."

"What about your brother? Could you not write him to send some money or a ticket?"

"No, no," the boy said hastily, wiping his nose on the ragged cotton sleeve of the oversized coat he wore despite the warmth of the day. "Mark sent me the first passage money. I could not tell him I lost it."

Pausing to point out the nose of *New World* just coming into view around a bend ahead, I casually inquired, "I thought his name was John."

"And so it is!" O'Reilly insisted, "John Mark, just like the Saints."

After this, the expression on the boy's face clouded. He leaned over the edge of the canoe and stared morosely into the water. I decided he could be no more than twelve years of age. Presently James O'Reilly fell asleep, leaving me to consider what caliber of elder brother would leave his adolescent sibling to make such a dangerous passage unaccompanied. I wondered about his family; all dead and gone. Had it been the Irish famine that had taken them? Or the cruel sea voyage? I was moved to pity. Thinking of my own upbringing in New York, I considered the question of my responsibility in seeing young James O'Reilly safely to California. It came to me that in similar circumstances I would hope some stranger would do the same for my kin. My raising weighed in heavily as I observed the waif. My practical father, who had no use for ragged Irish immigrants, would have booted young O'Reilly back into the gutter from whence he came. My dear Christian mother, who raised her children on stories of Samaritans and prodigals, would have scolded my father then gone out to fetch the child back. My decision to help the boy was made because my mother glowered down at me from the vapors of my imagination and overpowered my father's command that I use good judgment. It was a decision that I would occasionally regret.

CHAPTER 4

Wakeman took one look at the filthy, starving boy who accompanied me back to the steamer and sent him below for Elijah to feed. "Don't you want to hear his story?" I asked.

Waving his hand as if the matter was of complete indifference, Wakeman said, "Get to the important news. Is Jackson in Panama City and can he take the ship?"

So I explained about the reward posters, the hired mercenaries, and the apparent lack of civil authority. "If there were anyone in charge to appeal to, it would do you no good," I counseled. "Jackson obviously has most everyone in his pocket already, and the ones he doesn't own are cowed."

"So that's it then?" Wakeman grimaced. "You think we should go south and have *New World* haul guano for the Chileans?"

"Not at all," I said. "I just wanted you to know what we are up against. Here's my plan."

In a few moments I had outlined my thinking and Wakeman agreed. "With one proviso," he added. "Have the off-watch line the rail with fire axes and shovels. If you're wrong and they mean to board us, I intend to sell her dearly."

Wakeman's agreement to my scheme resulted in me being back in Panama City under cover of darkness that same night. There was not really any danger, although I did leave O'Reilly behind to continue getting fed almost to bursting.

My second visit to the Pacific port took me again to the Gato Negro, then on to the Tres Hermanos and the Sangre de Toro. I also paid calls on several of the hotels, which, in contrast to the cantinas, were owned and run by English-speakers: the Yankee Doodle, the George Washington, and the Constitution. I made the necessary arrangements and returned to Tabago at three in the morning.

Admittedly, I was more nervous by the time I got back to the ship than when I left. I was carrying gold and silver worth fifteen thousand dollars. I was tired too; that much coinage weighed close on a hundred pounds.

When we steamed into Panama City's harbor the following noon, the starboard side was lined with crewmen holding everything that could possibly be regarded as a weapon. Even 'Lijah was there with his meat cleaver. I was piloting. James O'Reilly was with me, since the wheelhouse was as near out of harm's way as there could be. I let him tend Scrimshaw for me. The black-beaked bird knew something was up. He squawked and shrilled at the top of his screech.

Wakeman stood on the foredeck in his best uniform.

His one hand rested lightly on the jackstaff and he looked as if our appearance in Panama was the outset of a pleasure cruise in Long Island Sound and we were about to pick up a load of sightseers.

The docks and the broken-down arcade were bustling, but the hubbub there was nothing to compare with the tumult that resulted when the captain signaled me to lay on the steam whistle. The way all the grog shops, hotels, and shops emptied, you would have thought that *New World*'s signal was the warning of an impending volcano and everyone wanted to get out of town.

We dropped the hook in six fathoms and Wakeman waved for me to join him in the launch. By the time we rowed ashore, a half dozen fights had already broken out among the hundreds of would-be miners who wanted to be first to speak with us.

"Back up and give me room," Wakeman said. The crowd did so. "All right, gentlemen," he said. "We have room for 350 passengers and have received three hundred deposits. Those of you who were sensible enough to take advantage of our offer last night will go aboard first, then we'll see about passage for a few more."

What was afoot here was this: In my nocturnal rounds of the Panama City establishments, I had spread the word that a steamer would be arriving the next day, destination California. I had been dressed in my officer's fig and my pitch was very simple: "Don't believe me if you're not inclined, but you will doom yourself to another month's stay in Panama."

Wakeman hired a whole flotilla of canoes to transport our new passengers aboard, after, I should add, they forked over the rest of their fares. The total of the collection amounted to ninety thousand dollars.

The orderly embarkation was interrupted by the not unexpected arrival of Sidney Jackson with his apes and his monkeys. A volley of rifle fire discharged into the air at the back of the crowd cleared a space for him to march down, flanked by Liam and Finn. "Wakeman," he intoned. "You are under arrest. I have papers here calling for the seizure and return of my ship to New York City."

An angry mutter began in the crowd. Jackson would have been better served had he said less and acted more circumspectly, but such was never his manner when he could be high-handed.

"Vhat about unser deposits?" a burly German demanded. "Vee vant California or de money beck."

Jackson tried to recover from his mistake. "I'll haul you to San Francisco," he said in the face of the rising agitation. "Don't worry," he tried to placate the mob.

Shaking his head, Wakeman smiled kindly. "I'm afraid not," he said. "If I raise my right arm above my head, those men you see on board the *World* have my order to up anchor and sail away. Your deposits are not refundable—my legal expenses, you see."

"What!" Jackson exploded. "You can't pirate my vessel twice!"

"I was about to say the same thing to you."

I watched Jackson's eyes carefully. Turning to the

henchmen standing at his side, the slightly built man was near to ordering us subdued. Wakeman's right hand crept slowly up to his lapel. "No!" the crowd bellowed. "California! My money! My passage! Out of my way!"

The sergeant of the guards foolishly raised his musket to his shoulder. A dozen prospectors wrenched it from his grip, broke it over his head, and left him unconscious on the cobblestones. The other mercenaries turned and fled. Liam and Finn regarded each other over Jackson's thinning hair. "Mister Jackson," Finn said, looking around at the angry faces of the throng, "let's be thinking this over."

The crowd hurrahed and stampeded past Jackson, pushing him aside as if he were a discarded banana peel.

Despite Wakeman's pitch about how limited the places were, by the time *New World* sailed there were over five hundred passengers stuffed into every conceivable space. Early bookings were three hundred dollars apiece; later we collected five hundred.

"Did you set the beggar boy ashore?" Wakeman demanded.

"No," I replied. "I thought we would give him passage to California."

"Who's going to pay his fare?"

"I thought he could bunk with me," I said.

"Not a chance," was the retort. "You and I are both giving up our cabins so ten paying customers can sleep in each. I'm taking over the cook's berth. You can fend for yourself."

"All right," I said grudgingly. "You're the captain.

But O'Reilly stays anyway. I'll pay his fare out of my share at the end of the voyage."

"Always picking up strays," Wakeman scolded with a disgusted look. "You never learn, do you?"

Captain Wakeman was all smiles after Panama City. Suddenly the danger of being arrested and deprived of the ship was gone. After thousands of miles of dodging British and American warships, all that danger was past. There was an American naval presence on the West Coast—exactly one ship: the sloop of war *Cyane*. Wakeman said that any day he and the *World* could not out-maneuver a sloop he would go back to whaling.

What was more, he had acquired paying passengers, which was exactly the use for which the steamer was designed. Of course, when Will Brown designed her, he had never envisioned quite the volume of customers that Wakeman packed aboard. As a river cruiser, *New World* had main deck space for a hundred seats and salon accommodations for a hundred more to dine or play cards. There were cabins to sleep forty at four to a room and deluxe staterooms on the top deck aft of the texas for a dozen more. All which calculations proved that the *World* was overloaded by double! Nor did this little mathematical exercise account for sleeping room or all the gear those prospectors brought aboard.

Never was seen such a conglomeration of nonsense in all the world. I stopped a New York Dutchman whose waistcoat did not quite stretch across his expansive belly. He was carrying a brass-belled blunderbuss that I imagine had last seen service with Captain John Smith two hundred years before. Nor was he the only man from whom I relieved a firearm. Soon the forward hold was bristling with rifles, fowling pieces, patented five-shooters and even a small cannon. I joked to O'Reilly that we could go ashore again and conquer Panama; then I was afraid to repeat the jest to Wakeman for fear he might want to try!

A Southern gentleman with an elegant mustache and a dueler's eye brought aboard a patented gold washing machine that looked like a scrubwoman's nightmare. His friend from Atlanta had a magnet in a bottle "guaranteed" to find the mother lode.

Two young men in long canvas coats over striped pantaloons next caught my attention. They were young enough to be sprightly, yet moved as if they were a hundred years of age. Their feet dragged with every step and their clothing clinked and clanked. Suspecting more weapons, I stopped them. "Here now," I said. "What's all this about?"

"It's the pieces of a cast-iron stove," the taller one declared.

"It's our livelihood," the other claimed. "We're going to open a restaurant."

There was even a tall, lean Yankee who had brought a granite tombstone already carved with his name; said he had no intention of being buried in an unmarked grave if his time ran out in California. I noted that he had not already filled in the date of his demise, however.

But just describing the sight of all the strange appliances, odd characters, and picturesque costumes does not do justice to the reality without reference to the sounds. Yankee twangs, Southern drawls, German throat clearing, French noses, and Irish brogues livened up the conversation. You could hear "pass the salt" in ten different languages at every meal.

Elijah, our cook, was sorely put to the test. Wakeman had promised that the passage money included all meals. There was ample cash to buy provisions in Mexican ports along the Gulf of Tehuantepec, but what an uproar was made over chow! Elijah, with O'Reilly helping as steward, took to standing in the galley door and flinging roast chickens into the mob. The fowls were torn limb-from-limb before one revolution of the paddle wheels had passed, and that is no exaggeration. Breakfast, consisting of porridge, bacon, and bread, was served at nine o'clock. Nine meant grab for whatever was within reach, because within two minutes it would all be gone. If a man wanted to sit down to eat, he got to the table an hour early, or did as many enterprising passengers did: They slept under it.

O'Reilly and I slept in the crew quarters aft in hammocks slung across the passageway. Wakeman had wanted to rent out that space too, but the crew indicated he would be sailing by himself thereafter and he relented. So it was that O'Reilly and I stood at the aft rail, a breathing space reserved for the sailors, just at sunset as I came off watch.

The western sky was all peach, fading up to pink, rising into purple. The air was sweet and the quiet blissful after the hectic day. "Do you think all these people will strike it rich?" O'Reilly asked me. "I mean, they all expect to go home with millions in gold."

I shrugged and scratched my chin where my beard was just beginning to grow in again. "Doubtful," I said. "Most of them will be lucky to get home alive."

"What about you?" he asked. "Will you turn prospector too?"

"Me? I'm a sailor. I'll make my living by *New World*, or a boat of my own some day, if I'm lucky. And I won't run off and leave my family like so many of these men have done."

"Do you have a family?" O'Reilly inquired.

"No, I meant when I have one," I said. "And if I stay in the West, I hope civilization shows up before I have a family. Did you ever see such an undisciplined horde of hooligans in your life?"

O'Reilly took Scrimshaw out of his cage and stroked the bird's head. The parrot fluffed his feathers and stretched his neck to be scratched. His eyes flashed with pleasure and he chuckled, "Hello, hello."

"Do you think it's because of the lack of women?" O'Reilly wondered aloud. "There is no female influence at all—not even one."

"I never gave it any thought," I said. "But maybe you're right. You seem genteel enough without a female present. Look how that parrot has taken to you, and he's a good judge of character. Well, I'm for bunk. We should reach Acapulco tomorrow. Ten more days to San Francisco."

The passengers of the *New World* were packed on board like sardines in a tin. While serving up porridge during morning mess, young James O'Reilly commented that the crew's quarters smelled like a barrel of old dead fish. With a disapproving eye cast upon certain grimy members of the entourage, James added, "Water everywhere and yet it seems there's not a bucket or a bar of soap to spare for washing. Did your mothers never teach you to wash your hands and face before you ate?"

The boy's remark was redressed with gibes from all hands that James's were perhaps too clean and that he had been seen dabbing vanilla behind his ears! "Don't he smell perty?" guffawed a gap-toothed stoker named Mazurky.

This last cut was nearly true. James splashed vanilla extract onto his kerchief and covered his nose with it whenever he descended into the engine room abyss of the crew quarters.

Mazurky sprang to his feet and, in imitation of James, held an oily rag to his nose and sashayed around the table. In a high falsetto he cried, "Lordy, lord! It stinks like a chamber pot down here!"

At the sound of the ruckus I descended in time to witness the scene. Mazurky gave James a shove into the arms of another of the black gang who planted a juicy kiss upon the boy's forehead. With an explosion of laughter, James was booted from one crew member to the next, falling at last into the arms of Elijah.

Now every man seemed pleased with the jest except for Elijah and young James. I was laughing along with the rest. I was, like the others, irritated by the mannerisms of the ragged boy. For one on the verge of manhood, he seemed altogether too fastidious. What the crew of *New World* lacked in personal cleanliness, James more than made up for. He retreated daily to the privacy of the hold and bathed in the dark. It was altogether unnatural.

The men were ready to go another round at the boy when Elijah bristled. "Leave the child alone!" bellowed the enormous black man.

The laughter died away quickly. Seldom had our cook displayed anything but a soft and gentle spirit. Now he took on the countenance of a giant bear rising up on its hind quarters to protect its young.

"Ah now, Elijah!" soothed Mazurky, reaching as if to grab the kid. "We're just havin' fun!"

Elijah slapped Mazurky's hand with a ladle and barked, "The boy's right! You smells like somethin' up and died!"

"That's your cooking!" called Mazurky.

There was nervous laughter among the crowd as Elijah's eyes widened with rage. He said to James, "Git on up outta here, child. Elijah's gonna take a few of these polecats on."

Now the crew was solemn. Chagrined, they dared not meet the gaze of Elijah who first upbraided them for their lack of hygiene and then for manhandling the boy. The net effect was to cause every one of the crew to resent James. It would have been better in the long run if Elijah had let him fight his own battles. That was not the case, however.

Elijah finished his tirade with this dire threat: "You ain't gonna get fed until you takes a bath. Not just a spit bath, neither. There's water enough to go around and I expects when we puts in for provision this afternoon you all goin' swimmin'. You gonna wash them filthy rags you call clothes before they putrefy and fall off. Make a man sick to smell you. So do it or else starve."

The threat was passed along to the reeking passengers as well. When *New World* anchored up at Acapulco, every man on board took Elijah at his word. Young, old, fat, skinny, short, and tall, every fellow peeled to the skin and swam for his supper.

Every man but one.

Carrying a bucket of potato peelings, James came up from the hold just as the ablutions were getting under way. I was balanced on the rail buck naked and poised to dive into the water when I heard a stifled cry behind me. Scrimshaw bobbed his head with joy and shouted, "Hullo! Hullo! Hullo!"

There was only one person on the ship whom Scrimshaw greeted with such delight. Glancing backwards I saw the ashen face of James as he emerged. I cried cheerfully, "Shed your duds and join us! The water's grand!"

The boy gawked in apparent horror at the state of undress of every man topside. His face went beet red. He spilled the bucket of peelings and fell back down the steps into the hold.

We were clean, at his instigation, and yet he did not join in our frolic.

James kept to himself even more. To my immense irritation, he did not look me directly in the eye from that day onward. On occasion I caught him sneaking glances at me. He would blush and turn away the instant I faced him or attempted conversation. It was as if he had some terrible secret that he did not want me to find out. Perhaps he feared I would throw him to the sharks. I was tempted to do so.

His odd behavior reinforced my sense that James O'Reilly was a liar and a thief and probably on the run from the law. I considered wringing the truth out of the wretch, but restrained myself because of the fondness that Elijah seemed to have for the boy.

I consoled myself that the *World* was full of odd characters and that most of us were on the run from something or someone.

CHAPTER 5

Our arrival in San Francisco was not what you might call auspicious, even though it first appeared to be. As we sighted the headlands that marked the Golden Gate and entered the bay that was the object of our eighteen-thousand-mile journey, a signal cannon was fired, flags hoisted atop what we learned to call Telegraph Hill, and a bonfire lighted in honor of our appearance. As we rounded the eastern curve of the peninsula and entered a boat basin crammed with the masts of sailing ships, hundreds of Californians lined the shore, waving and cheering. This looked all to the good.

What soon became apparent was that what we had taken to be a welcoming celebration was actually a shindig in honor of Independence Day. The smoke we saw was just San Francisco having one of its usual conflagrations, caused this time by a bottle rocket. The city, if such a grand title can be applied to a collection of tents, adobe hovels, and driftwood shacks, caught fire near the docks and an east wind merrily pushed the flames up and over the hills.

A great clamor arose from our passengers to be set ashore. Was this because of their civic-mindedness in wanting to help quench the blaze? Not on your tintype! They wanted to get ashore so as to buy supplies for mining before all the foodstuffs and equipment burned up!

Captain Wakeman directed me to dock *New World* next to the hull of a sailing ship named the *Fanny*. The *Fanny* looked deserted and derelict. Her masts were gone and the planking of her top deck appeared to be loose, as if pulled up on purpose. Our passengers swarmed ashore without so much as a thank-you; possibly they were as heartily sick of our company as we were of theirs.

Watching them go with a scornful expression on his face, Wakeman laughed when he turned to me. "They'll be back," he said. "They don't know it yet, but they are still 150 miles from the diggings and the easiest and fastest way to do the first hundred of that distance is the *New World*. Rafer," he said, turning to me and squaring up his cap. "Till Mister Brown arrives, I'm in charge of seeing that the *World* makes a profit. I'm going ashore to inquire about getting tickets printed and handbills. Meantime, you're in command. You're captain. Get a chart of the river for your first trip to Sacramento City."

"And when will that be?" I asked.

"Day after tomorrow," Wakeman concluded blithely. "Don't forget to coal up, have Olson swap the boiler tubes out, jack down the crank and grease it, and see what you can do about hiring a standby pilot." He turned to leave without a wink; he really thought I could accomplish all he said in forty-eight hours. "By the way," he added. "In your spare time, see what the competition is up to."

After I communicated Wakeman's orders to the engineer, I went ashore myself and made the acquaintance of a real salt by the name of Fouratt. He was short and grizzled, stooped slightly at the shoulders, and was dark complected and weather-beaten. In sum, he was the human illustration of the stumpy briar pipe that was wedged between his teeth. Like me, he had come west by ship round the Horn. He had already taken a half dozen brigs, sloops, and schooners upriver to Sacramento under sail. I was impressed. It was quite a feat of seamanship to navigate the twists and turns of a river with only the wind for power to overcome the current.

"Perty ship," he growled, gesturing with the stem of his pipe at *New World* as we returned aboard. A gang of workmen moved onto the hulk of *Fanny*, and from the pry bars they carried, I figured them for a salvage crew. They covered the deck with canvas and commenced removing the planks.

"Do you know where I can come by a chart of the river?" I asked Fouratt.

"Right here," he said. "Got one with me."

I looked him over from stem to stern, but no sign of a roll of map or fold of paper could I see.

"Bring me your logbook and somethin' to write with," he demanded. When I returned a minute later with the requested implements, he leaned over the anchor windlass and began to draw. "Now this first stretch is no bother till you get above Benecia," he said. "When you come to the next point of land dividing the river, take the north fork; t'other leads to Tuleberg." He sketched curves, bends, narrows, and false channels, all the while keeping up a nonstop commentary.

"Hold on," I interrupted when I could. (He had paused to relight the foul pipe.) "Don't you *have* a chart?"

"What have I been doin' here? The river runs down to the bay, don't it? How can you go wrong if you keep to the main channel, and I'm showin' you how to do that."

And he did; over a hundred miles of waterway, covering several pages of the log. On some unnamed bends he wrote comments like "shoal water here, hug the left bank," and "big snag midchannel, hidden at high water."

When he was through, I offered him the position of relief pilot. His reply was as surprising as his memory: he laughed out loud and said, "Mebbe."

Back at the gangplank I asked him the other question that had been on Wakeman's mind, as well as my own. "What about other steamers?"

"There's *Antelope* and *Senator*," he ticked off the boats with his stubby pipe on his equally stubby fingers, "and *Goliath*—that's all of consequence. 'Course, you're tied up right next to one."

"Where?" I demanded, looking round me. No other steamship could I see and *Fanny* looked ready to sink. In fact, she was sinking. Right there at the dock.

As Fouratt watched with his arms folded across his chest, I stared in amazement as the hull of the sailing ship dropped away, gurgling downward into the bay. But the canvas cover did not drop with the sinking ship. The working party, none of whom looked dismayed at the loss, stripped back the cover to reveal the form of a steamboat. She was minus her stack and paddle wheels, but there was no mistaking her form.

"There's your newest competition," Fouratt said. "My ship—the *Wheeler*; brought round the Horn inside *Fanny* like Jonah in the belly of the whale. See you later," he added. "Good luck to you."

Now it would seem that the day had already had surprises in plenty, but there was one more in store. I went below to gather my belongings to move them back to my own cabin in the texas. When I got to the crew's berth, I found a young red-haired woman, slim and comely and about eighteen years of age, admiring Scrimshaw. The normally suspicious parrot was perched on her arm, allowing her to tickle him.

"Beg pardon, miss," I said. "I didn't know you came aboard. If you're seeking passage upriver, we won't be leaving for several days."

The beautiful girl only smiled and said nothing. But there was something about that smile that was familiar. Scrimshaw was fluffing and pinpointing his eyes. I certainly agreed with his taste, but was surprised he was so taken with a total stranger.

Then she called him by name and her voice told me

all. "You're . . . you're . . . O'Reilly," I stuttered. "You're a . . ."

"Girl," she finished for me. "Yes, Rafer, that's true. I'm sorry about the deception, but being alone with five hundred men, it seemed the wisest course. My name *is* Jamie O'Reilly, by the way. I am a married woman, come to seek my husband."

I studied her as I had Fouratt; from stem to stern, that is. A blush climbed her throat to her freshly scrubbed cheeks. When I realized I was staring, I was embarrassed in my turn and apologized. "Your clothes," I said at last. "You had nothing with you. How?"

"Elijah," she explained. "Working beside him in the kitchen, he caught on right away, but kept my confidence. He went ashore and returned with these clothes for me."

She departed then, leaving me gaping after her and wondering about steamships hiding inside leaky old brigs and beautiful young women camouflaged as boys. California was surely a land of surprises.

Standing at the rail of the hurricane deck, I watched Jamie O'Reilly cut a swath through the teeming sea of men on the docks. Hats of every size and description were doffed as she passed. Although uneasy at her departure, I comforted myself in the fact that the thousand scruffy miners in her path gaped with astonishment and awe. It was plain from the look of her that Jamie was not one of the females making a living in the back rooms of the Barbary Coast saloons. Mrs. O'Reilly carried herself with the dignity of a queen rather than the awkward shyness of a farm girl just off the boat from Ireland. Hoisting the hem of her skirt up from the mud and tobacco juice, she nodded regally as caps were removed and sweeping bows made.

I half expected some silk-caped gambler to toss his cloak onto the ground for her to tread upon. Within my vision, however, no man played Sir Walter Raleigh to her Queen Elizabeth. As she vanished around a corner, I felt a pang of regret. How had I not noticed that she was entirely the opposite gender to me?

Exhaling loudly, I turned away and found myself face-to-face with Elijah. He scowled past me out at the swarm of bearded and mustached faces.

"You let her go." His comment was an accusation.

"I could not keep her from it, could I?" I shrugged off his disapproval.

"You let her go out there alone to look for her man?"

"If she doesn't find the one she's looking for, there will be plenty of others."

"Don't talk 'bout Mizz Jamie that way, Rafer. She's a good woman."

"She may be good, but seems to me you're the only one on board the *New World* who had any notion about the woman part of that equation."

He rubbed his ebony cheek as if choosing his words carefully. "Don't know how you missed it. Writ all over her face. She was a marigold in a pigsty, that's all. Writ all over the way she moved and how she talk. Skeert of menfolks. Or couldn't you tell?"

"I thought she was just . . . just a peculiar . . . boy."

Elijah harrumphed in disgust. "Peculiar alright. You didn't notice the way she was a-lookin' at you?"

"She never looked at me at all."

"That's right. She looked everywhere but where you was."

"So what?"

"You're a bigger fool than I figured, Rafer."

"You tend to your beans and bacon."

"It's your fault she's gone alone into the streets of Sodom. No money. No friends."

I growled defensively, "She made it this far without either. And I'll tell you something else—Jamie O'Reilly will have every miner in California thinking she's the Virgin Mary returned to earth in a vision of glory. She walked through that mob of rowdies easier than a tornado whipping through a cane field. She should have put on skirts long ago, Elijah. Dress her up in womany gear and every man she meets will fall down and worship."

Elijah eyed me with some disdain. "That's exactly why Mizz Jamie did not let you know who she was, nor what."

I turned away, gazing solemnly at the undulating crowds. Like every other two-legged male varmint on the West Coast, I would have enjoyed falling at the feet of Jamie O'Reilly.

"She could have traveled up the Delta with us, then

gone on to find her husband in the gold camps. She did not have to jump ship."

"You thinkin' of her husband, eh?" Elijah laughed sarcastically. "And what fare would you ask if she stayed on board? Yessir, Mizz Jamie never looked you in the eye. 'Fraid of what you might see, I reckon. You'd have seen the truth alright. And if you had know'd she took a shine to you, you'd of been on her like a duck on a June bug. She's a married woman. A good woman. So she lit out."

Elijah was right about me. If I had known, I would have put forth my best effort to win her heart entirely. When it came to fine women, fine horse flesh, and fine ships, I had weaknesses. I did not admit this to Elijah, however. Instead, I rebutted, "Her husband is some kind of fool to leave her to shift for herself. He deserves to lose her. A sweet vessel like that can't sail for long without a captain."

"Reckon she was sure what kind of man you was, Rafer. Steal a ship. Steal the heart of another man's wife? Anyhow, that's why she decided she's gonna find her own way back to that husband of hers."

I returned to the wheelhouse in time to receive an additional scolding from Scrimshaw. The bird spread his wings and gave a great shriek of unhappiness. His eyes pinpointed and he danced back and forth on his perch as if to tell me he did not want Mrs. O'Reilly to leave him behind.

I said to the bird, "You knew it all along, you traitor. You and your señoritas. But you didn't tell me."

"Bad bird, bad bird," Scrimshaw returned. He was talking to me.

Mrs. O'Reilly remained in my thoughts only briefly after that. I considered my encounter with her like the brief glint of sun on the back of a large rainbow trout darting through a stream. The same moment I knew she was there it was too late to catch her. Now she was gone. I considered that I would never meet up with her again. I turned my thoughts away from fishing and on to the business of setting the *New World* in order after her long sea voyage.

As for young Mrs. O'Reilly, she had no time to look back or think of me at all. She had a mission to accomplish and now I was just a small completed step in its fulfillment. A sense of exhilaration filled her. She imagined that her beloved Danny might have stood in this very spot upon his arrival and witnessed the same bizarre scenes now before her.

Leaving the waterfront, she paused a moment to observe the raw new city of San Francisco. Deserted ships had been dragged ashore and planted in the clay to become hotels, saloons, and bawdy houses. Prows jutted onto the street and signs hung from the masts declaring the type of business transactions held within. Doors had been cut through hulls that had kept back the heaviest Cape Horn seas. Now waves of humans passed freely through to buy shovels or beans or whiskey or to rent a woman for an hour or so.

A cluster of three painted ladies lounged outside the door of the Nantucket Hotel. The structure had once been a whaling vessel. It left the slaughter off Lahaina Roads, Hawaii, to sail direct to California when news of the gold strike arrived. From the look of the hull the captain had not stopped to anchor when he reached port, but had driven his ship aground and jumped off to run all the way to the Sierra. Now, Nantucket suffered the indignity of two additional clapboard stories perched above the deck where the masts had been. The American flag drooped forlornly from a flagpole that had once been the mainmast.

The painted ladies called to the new arrivals, "New in town?"

"Long time at sea?"

"This is where you'll get a taste of home."

Jamie gaped at the performance as yet another scantily clad woman draped herself out a hatch and called down to two pug-faced twin brothers. The men were a perfect match from their weather-scarred features to their flaming red hair, except that one wore a blue shirt and the other red.

"Two for the price of one, boys!" the harlot called, gesturing at a ladder leaning on the side of the ship.

Standing near to Jamie, the red shirt said to the blue in an Irish brogue, "Can ya picture a walla with such a one? She's ugly as that sow in Darnley's sty."

Jamie thought that this comment on appearances was

the pot calling the kettle black. After all, it was seldom that she had seen two such homely men as these.

The other twin agreed with his brother's assessment. "Aye, and twice as fat. From the look of her she's got a litter of shoats squealin' at her feet as well."

A passing teamster observed the disgust on their faces and shouted down from his wagon, "There's ten thousand men for ever' woman on this coast, boys. Soon enough you'll think the Nantucket women are all fair and that they sing like larks!"

"Never!" called back the blue shirt. His eye fell on Jamie, who was smiling at the exchange.

Red shirt noticed her at the same moment. "But look here, Mike! Now here is something to write home about."

"As if you could write!" the blue shirt snorted. His knapsack slung on his shoulder, he strolled toward Jamie. "Are there any more where you come from, darlin'?"

Jamie raised her chin. "You should know. By the sound of your speech you're a couple of bog-hearted micks from the black Tyrone. Church of Ireland, I'm guessin'."

The brothers clapped arms about one another's shoulders and stood before her so she could not pass. "It's Saint Bridget. A Catholic whore come to work the docks of California."

Jamie felt her temper rise. "I'm Mrs. O'Reilly to you spawn. And you'll mind your tongues. The Association is not all starvin' back in Ireland."

"A feisty one, Mike!" grinned the red shirt. "We've hung a few of your papist relatives in our day. Your husband here, is he?"

Jamie tried to pass but they moved to block her way. "Let me go," she said archly. "I'm meeting my husband."

The blue shirt grabbed her wrist and squeezed. "Married are you? Where's your wedding band then?"

She jerked her hand away and did not tell him that she had sold it to buy food in Panama. "Let go of me, you unmannered Orange baboon! By all the saints I'll—"

Red shirt grabbed her around the waist and pulled her against him. He laughed and his breath was stinking with whiskey. "I've always had a taste for papist girls."

"You're drunk," she said, trying to get free. "Let me go. You've had a drop too much."

"What do you say, girl? I'll pay you same as I'd pay that sow in the Nantucket porthole. Right here. What do you say?"

Struggling, Jamie opened her mouth to cry out. Red shirt clapped his hand over her lips, then pressed her tightly against his chest so no one passing could see her terror. He laughed at the game.

A crowd gathered. Those in the half-moon of spectators around her were jeering with expectation of a show. After all, what would a respectable woman be doing so near the Nantucket? Surely this fresh-faced girl was no more than something new to the waterfront stable of loose women.

Blue shirt raised his arms and faced the mob. He

shouted, "What do you say, gentlemen? Care to watch? Or have a go at her yourselves?"

A cheer rose up. Coins hit Jamie on the back. She felt her consciousness slipping away. The fingers of her attacker pressed fiercely into her cheek. She prayed but there was no one to help her.

Above them a female voice boomed down. "Let her go, you dog! If you want a little action, get it where it's welcome!"

Red shirt turned his face up toward the woman in the hatchway. "We're bringin' you business, madam." He staggered closer toward the hull of the ship. "It's thankful you should be! We're getting rid of your competition. And after this there'll not be a man in the crowd who is not in need of your assistance. You'll be owin' us a commishun."

The woman stroked her chin. "I don't hold with independents and that's a fact. If she's going to work my territory she'll pay for it. But not in the street. It ain't seemly. Don't set a good example for those of us in a legitimate business. Bring her in, boys. You'll have a free room to use. Just the brothers. The rest of you wait your turns outside."

The crowd applauded and shuffled toward the Nantucket. Moments later Jamie was dragged, kicking, through the rough cut opening into the lantern lit interior of the hull. The place was decked out like a pub with a bar across the back where an enormous Samoan islander wiped shot glasses with a dirty rag. He barely glanced up. His broad face was a dark scowl and he stood with his halo of bushy hair bowed beneath the low ceiling. The tattooed native was much a part of the setting. Decorated with paintings of islands and breaching whales, the wood paneling of the Nantucket still reeked of burned whale blubber.

Jamie's mind was shrieking, *I'm a married woman! Let me go! This is a mistake!* But her words were muffled by the tight grip across her face.

The stout madam appeared on the steps that led up to the rooms. She said to five inadequately dressed women who lounged around the bar, "Don't let anyone else pass until I give the word, girls."

Shooting the brothers a stern look she remarked, "Twins, are you?"

Red shirt panted eagerly, "Aye. Born the same day."

The proprietress screwed up her face and mumbled, "Should've been drowned at birth."

"What's that, ma'am?" asked blue shirt.

Managing a smile, the madam replied, "I said we have found you a comfortable berth." Snapping her fingers, she called the barkeep from behind his station. "Tafua, show these brothers some island hospitality." For just a moment the woman allowed her eyes to linger with pity on Jamie.

The giant Tafua grinned with gleaming white teeth as he removed a harpoon from its pegs behind the bar. He touched his finger to the tip of the iron spearhead. "Madam don't like no ugly haole boys steal her thunder. I think I like kill you both. Stick you through like kalua pig, an' feed you to the shark out there in the bay. Plenty big sharks, too."

The Irish brothers each twittered with identical nervous giggles. Red shirt still clasped Jamie's mouth. "He's joking, ain't he?"

Madam grinned. "I don't think so." The wood of the steps groaned beneath her weight as she descended. "Now let the girl go."

Red shirt gasped and flung Jamie away as if she had burned him. She fell at the feet of the great Tafua.

Blue shirt croaked, "We . . . we're just . . . just . . ."

Tafua made as if to harpoon him. "Shut your mouth, haole pig. I kill you right now." Jabbing the weapon at their terrified faces, Tafua backed the two into a corner and held them at bay with the threat that if they spoke or moved he would skewer them instantly.

Jamie sat up slowly and managed to find her voice. "Thank you. Thank you so much. I was afraid I was . . . I'm a married woman, you see. Come to find my husband!"

Madam sniffed with amusement. "He might have been here, but there are so many, honey, we don't ask their names." She swept her fleshy hand over the heads of her girls. "Anybody seen her husband?"

A chorus of voices replied, "Not me."

"Don't think so."

"What did he look like, honey?"

Helping Jamie to her feet, the proprietress touched the girl's cheek. "You're a sweet little thing. You'd draw a crowd, but I can see you ain't int'rested in employment."

Jamie's eyes brimmed. "I am looking for my husband, you see . . ."

"You said that." Madam glanced at Tafua. "You'll have to take care of those two after dark. Can't let them go noising around San Francisco that they didn't get a friendly welcome at Nantucket."

"I kill them good." Tafua grinned first, then scowled and took a warlike stance. The two brothers groaned and cringed and squatted on the floor in abject terror.

Jamie blinked at the scene in disbelief. "Will he?"

Patting her on the shoulder, the madam led Jamie to the opposite side of the room where she confided, "There's a British ship leaving tonight for England, by way of South Africa. I'll let word get to the captain I've got a couple of deserters off another British vessel. He is one mean kahuna, that gent. If he don't hang them first, he'll certain flog them, which they deserve—then work them like the dogs they are. The British navy can sort it out when they reach England in a year or two."

Jamie was relieved that there would be no murders on her behalf, although a flogging seemed most appropriate. "I . . . I don't know quite what to do after this."

"There, there, honey. You wait in my quarters till eight bells or so. I'll have Tafua escort you to a nice gentleman who will know just how to help."

After nightfall Tafua rowed the Irish ruffians, bound and gagged, out to the British frigate. They were gratefully received since a number of the crewmen had deserted for the goldfields. Tafua was paid the handsome reward of a gold sovereign for each. This put into the head of the Samoan that he would be on the lookout for any more hooligans who needed transportation away from California. The way he saw matters, the grinning Samoan, the needy skipper, and California would all be the better for his services.

Upon returning to the Nantucket, Tafua reported to Madam that all had gone smoothly. When Madame put out her meaty palm and asked for the certain reward, Tafua placed one coin in her hand.

"Only one, Tafua? Captain Blanton has been more generous in times past."

Tafua shrugged. "When Tafua harpoon a whale he get the gold piece off the mast. This time two. I split 'em with you or go find another ship."

Madam consented. Tafua was too valuable an asset to let go. His mammoth presence served as both deterrent and highly visible warning to any patrons who became too rowdy.

Standing in the shadow of this giant, Jamie also had a firm sense of security. Bidding Madam and the girls farewell, Jamie left for the Mission of San Francisco, which lay just on the other side of the hills from the waterfront.

Like a servant to a princess, Tafua carried the lantern before her. In Jamie's perception, however, she trailed in

Tafua's wake like a small fish behind a whale. Although the raucous nightly celebrations of the Barbary Coast were in full swing, not one drunk let his lustful gaze linger on Jamie lest the wrath of the tattooed Samoan be loosed.

It was near midnight when they reached the quiet walls of the great adobe mission. New arrivals slept side by side beneath the shelter of the porticoes.

Jamie was bone weary and chilled from the foggy breeze that swept up from the bay. She nodded gratefully as Tafua rang the bell to the inner courtyard.

There was no reply and Jamie said quietly, "I'll sleep here. No one will trouble me here at the gates of the mission."

"You don't know them haole dogs. Why you think priests lock up gates? Tafua could fill whole big ship with haole pigs. Madam say I take you straight to Father Patrick. You don't go no place else." Tafua repeated the command of his employer as though Jamie had no say in the matter at all. He pounded heavily against the thick planks of the gates and shouted, "Father Patrick! Here is Tafua! From Madam at Nantucket. I got a girl for you!"

This cry raised the heads of the sleepers and evoked an immediate response from the inner sanctum. The bolts slid back and the barriers opened wide to reveal the angry face of a brown-robed Franciscan friar who was nearly as round as the Samoan, yet half his height.

Tafua clapped the priest on both shoulders. "Ah! Here he is! Father Patrick! You see what I brung you?"

The joyful greeting was not returned.

"Tafua! By all the saints! Keep your voice down. You'll have half the city thinking I'm doing business with you!"

Crossing herself, Jamie said in a quiet voice, "Bless you, Father! I am Missus Jamie O'Reilly, late of County Cork and new arrived from the East in search of my husband. I am in desperate need of shelter and comfort."

Friar Patrick, who had come from Ireland to California thirty years before, took the lantern from Tafua and lowered it so the light shone full on Jamie's face. "It's plain you're a respectable woman. Perhaps a foolish one, to come so far and to such a place as this. How came you to be in the company of this heathen?"

Tafua drew himself up. "Tafua keep her safe from haole pig-dogs."

"It's true," Jamie hastened to agree. "I was accosted by evil-minded Orangemen nearly the moment I was out of sight of the ship. This fellow saved me from a desperate fate. The madam protected me until it was safe for me to come to you. Will you help me?"

Sighing, the priest stepped aside. "Come in then. Tafua, don't be thinking you'll get a reward from me. Your reward will be from heaven's King the moment you forsake your heathen ways and enter true grace as we have spoken many times."

"Aye, Father." Tafua nodded solemnly. "Someday Tafua gonna get saved. But Tafua ain't through killing and being too sinful first. Tafua come back when he old man like you and don't like no more fun."

"You'll be hung before that, Tafua." Father Patrick

clucked his tongue and closed the gates and locked them. He inclined his head toward the dark corridor that led to the sanctuary. The new arrivals followed in silence. At the door of the church the priest held up his hand to stop Tafua's entry. The Samoan obeyed, crouching down with his back against the cold adobe. Almost instantly Tafua was snoring.

The priest touched Jamie's elbow and ushered her into the sanctuary where rows of votive candles flickered to illuminate the vast interior in a soft light.

Jamie crossed herself and then, without warning, she burst into tears. "Oh, Father! He was last in Nevada City! I've come such a long way to find Danny, and now I fear I'll never find him and that perhaps I've lost myself in all the long journey!" She buried her face in her hands.

Clearing his throat, the priest commented kindly, "Well, Missus O'Reilly. You're not much more than a girl. I'll warrant it will not take long to find yourself again. But as for your husband, California is a vast place. The gold camps are my parish. I travel from place to place to offer comfort for the souls of God's children. Nevada City is on my circuit. I do not recall the name of any Danny O'Reilly."

"What shall I do then? Where shall I go? If you do not remember him, then where can he be?"

"Be comforted, child. If I do not remember the lad, then that means I have not performed last rights over him."

Jamie raised her head. "I do find comfort in that. Unless he's died unshriven and unknown."

"Many men have met untimely ends here, but God's children are never unknown. The fact that you have made it safely thus far is proof of that." He led her gently to a long bench and bade her sit. "Can you cook?"

"Danny would not have wed me if I was not a good cook."

"Good cooking draws a crowd. Would you like to travel into the hills with me, girl? Nevada City? I've got a Mexican drover who serves up pig swill for supper every day. It would be good to eat something that does not fracture my teeth. I am treated kindly everywhere I travel. You'll be safe, that is certain."

"This fearsome day has become an answer to every prayer I prayed these long months."

"All things work together for our good. For those who love the Lord, every road leads to heaven. Even a very hard road. There is great solace in that, I find. Now, I'll fetch you a blanket. The bench is hard, but you can sleep here beneath the watchful eyes of Jesus and all the saints."

One last surge of panic overwhelmed Jamie as she considered that she was so very close to finding Danny. "What if he isn't in Nevada City? What if . . ." Her voice trailed away.

"Turn from worry to praise before you close your eyes this night, Jamie O'Reilly. A cheerful heart is the best offering we can give to God. He will guide you. By morning, I wager, you'll no longer feel lost. We begin our journey at daybreak."

CHAPTER 6

My first trip upriver as captain of *New World* was made on July 15, 1850. My destination was Sacramento City; my cargo, three hundred miners who paid thirty dollars apiece to make the trip. Wakeman had also somehow arranged a load of picks, shovels, and other mining gear.

The Sacramento River is neither wide nor particularly swift. Its main hazards aside from snags are the tule fog in winter and other river traffic. The steamships did not own the river then and maneuvering to allow for sailboats was one of my biggest challenges.

One of the tricks of river piloting was that a skipper must know his location at all times, in all weather, and under all circumstances. Sudden maneuvers were called for in order to avoid smashing a scow loaded with garden truck into toothpicks and peelings. Given that circumstance, the pilot had to know immediately what the options were. Was there enough water to hug the bank, or was it necessary to put the helm hard over and shoot across the channel? Should he back the engine or come ahead full?

The only way to learn the river was to sail it until it was as familiar as your own face. The trick for a newcomer like myself was to avoid making any deadly mistakes until the stream was as plain blindfolded as in broad daylight. In other words, I needed to become as canny with the channel as Enos Fouratt.

Fortunately, Enos Fouratt was as friendly as he was given to teasing. He was, in fact, the captain of the newly reborn steamship *Wheeler* and he really did carry all the twists and turns of the river in his head. But he did not expect me to absorb all the information about rocks and shoals, false channels, and bluff reefs in one session with a handdrawn map.

Instead he made me a generous offer: In exchange for free passage upriver to transact some business in Sacramento City, Fouratt would deadhead along and "learn me proper."

Crossing San Francisco Bay and entering the estuary of the Sacramento took no great skill. A child could pilot after having been pointed toward a few landmarks. Indeed, even upriver for miles, at least as far as Rio Vista, there were no intricate moves required. Fouratt smoked his pipe and chatted about gold fever and how the population had changed since he came west. "Don't believe the Bear Flag War would have got settled so easy if the Mexicans had known about the gold. No sirree! Nobody much wanted the headache of governing California, so they said to Fremont and them others, 'Take her and welcome.' Look here! Don't you bet they kick themselves now? Mark me, they'll try and take it back one day!"

Only two years had elapsed between when the control of the Pacific Coast passed into the hands of the United States and the discovery of gold by Sutter's mill foreman James Marshall. Two more years had passed since then and California was already on the verge of statehood.

New World was on the verge of Grand Island and two large channels loomed ahead. "Now let me take her, if you please Mister Maddox," Fouratt said formally. "Yonder port channel is Steamboat Slough. It has water enough and is shorter and straighter to Sacramento City, but it bypasses some settlements on the main course. Which'll it be?"

"The main river this trip, I think," I said. "Shortcuts for later."

"Aye, aye," he agreed. Setting the *World* in her marks between a prominent cottonwood tree on one bank and a flagpole on the other, we passed the first crossroads of the stream.

For the next two hours Fouratt "learned me the river." He showed me knobby earthen knolls that featured as navigation aids, saying that they were ancient Indian burial mounds. At another bend he instructed me to crowd the far shore, even though the channel appeared to follow the nearer. "Sunken schooner midstream," he said. "Next winter's flood will shift her and some boat's belly will educate us about her new position."

When we rounded the curve above Andrus Island, Fouratt gestured at a white speck in the distance. "What do you suppose that is?" he inquired.

I studied the luminous spot by eye, then glassed it and replied, "Looks to be a blockhouse or some such."

"Trick of the light," he said. "Keep watching."

As the *World*'s course took her nearer the object, it appeared to shrink in size. Its lines remained those of a white cube, but just what it signified I could not make out.

Finally we closed enough for the pale structure to resolve itself into a painted fence enclosing a rectangle of earth no more than four by six. "A grave?" I asked. Then looking around at the bulrushes, the muddy banks, and the complete absence of humankind, I added, "Way out here?"

Fouratt nodded grimly. "A story goes with it." As if his tobacco habit and tale-telling were inextricably linked, as soon as he uttered the word *story*, his hand stole toward his pouch and he recharged his pipe before commencing. "Body of a man was found here," he said. "Young man, pale haired. Irish, belike. Horribly marred he was, run over by a paddle wheel. It was not known whether that killed him or happened after, but no matter; he was stone dead either way. Boat crew buried him where you're looking."

My mind leaped at once to young Jamie O'Reilly's husband. But no; there were many sons of Ireland in the gold camps. I was still unclear about Fouratt's mysterious air. "Drunken miners must fall over some," I said.

Fouratt agreed. "More than should happen," he said ominously.

"But what is the secret?"

"The grave," Fouratt said, gesturing toward the barricade. "Newspapers spread the word of the finding of the body, but no one claimed to know the man. Then, less than a fortnight later, the fence appeared around the mound, some time between dusk and dawn."

"And no one admitted doing it? But why not? Surely it was a good, Christian act to provide a decent resting place?"

"There you've spliced it," Fouratt grunted around his pipe stem, slapping his hands together and frightening Scrimshaw into squawking. "Why wouldn't one admit it, unless the deed was by way of atoning for a guilty conscience?"

"You mean, the man was murdered and his killer's remorse led to the fencing of the grave?"

"Now mind," Fouratt said, "I do not claim to know what lies in the hearts of men. But I know this much: Mine is the crew that buried the man, and these are the eyes that were first laid on yonder enclosure." We passed much of the remainder of the voyage in silent thought until it came time for Fouratt to coach me in the procedures for docking at the Sacramento City wharf.

There were a great many things that demanded my attention in Sacramento City. I had to arrange to have

New World refueled, I had to see that our galley was restocked and the boat spruced up, I needed to dispatch Nuck Gutterson and two others of the crew to tack handbills all over Sacramento's oak trees and so forth. And in the midst of all these necessities, my mind insisted on thinking about her: Jamie O'Reilly, of course.

It is said the sea is a jealous mistress and the notion that ships are female is universally regarded as fact. *New World* was my true love, but for all that, I could not help thinking about Mrs. O'Reilly. I reminded myself that she was married and devoutly so; she had traveled around half the world and endured many hardships in order to seek her mate. Her devotion and her spunk made her admirable. Taken in package with all the rest of her qualities, she was irresistible.

Just the sort of thinking that drove me to keep as busy as possible.

I took myself off to the local newspaper, the *Sacramento Independent*, to arrange for advertisements to appear in the weekly paper. Being a riverman, I studied the levees that protected the business district with a practiced eye. I concluded that a three-foot rise in the river would inundate the town and turn the dirt streets into quagmires. As a sailor, I like the properties water possesses, but I also insist that it stay where it properly belongs.

In any case, the offices of the *Independent* would not be in danger. Being completely innocent of foundation, the shanty in which freedom of the press resided in this portion of the West would most likely float free and relocate to San Francisco Bay.

The business manager, editor in chief, local correspondent, and typesetter all rose to greet me, and he was a real gentleman. Despite being a one-horse operation and therefore fidgety about long conversations, Alfred Squires was a Southerner. He had been transported to California, not by floodwaters, but by the rising tide of gold fever.

When gold nuggets did not really call his name from pockets in the streambeds, Squires paid to have a press shipped out from Charleston, South Carolina, and went back to the business he knew best: rabble-rousing. All this information was in the future, however, on the occasion of my first visit.

"A naval officer," he proclaimed in bell-like tones when I entered his shack. "What brings you to this citadel of truth and justice?"

When I explained who I was and what I had come for, he stripped off his sleeve protectors and eyeshade, as if he needed to appear properly clothed in order to change from printer to director of advertisements. "It is high time we had some competition around here on the water," he said. "Thirty dollars apiece for passage to Frisco is highway robbery. And collecting one silver dollar each for freighting bricks! Outrageous!" This editorial opinion left me little to say, since those were the identical rates Wakeman was charging, at least to begin with. Fortunately, Squires, having delivered his estimation, was now ready to conduct business. "What do you want the copy to say?"

"We will be running a regular schedule, leaving San Francisco at ten in the morning Monday, Wednesday, and Friday, and departing Sacramento City for the bay at the same hour on the other days except Sunday."

"And what shall I say is the steaming time?"

"We expect to make the passage in under seven hours."

Squires snorted. "One hundred miles in seven hours means averaging—"(here he paused and stared at the hole in the ceiling, which I took to be intended for a stovepipe when he could afford a stove)—"Fourteen knots, including stops. You must be mistaken. The fastest time on the river so far is over eight hours, set just two months ago by *Goliath*."

I grinned and said, "In that case we will soon be providing newsworthy copy, wouldn't you say?"

"Indeed, sir, indeed! And a good change of pace from all these stories about disappearing prospectors gone on binges, no doubt. Now, about this advertisement. May I have discretion to word it as I see fit?"

"Use your professional judgment," I agreed.

"Thank you," he responded with a courtly bow. "Part of my composing case sank in last winter's storms. The streets of Sacramento may be enriched by my words, but it has left me deucedly short of *t*s, *r*s, and *h*s."

On my first trip back down from Sacramento City I got a taste of river piloting, California style. There was a sailors' hangout on the wharf called The Corposant, which is a kind of eerie lightning observed at sea. I suppose the owner called it that to advertise his familiarity with things nautical, or perhaps it was to discourage non-sailors from patronizing his dive. Or most likely of all, it referred to the effect produced on the brain of those who consumed the rotgut grog he sold there.

The *World* was being wooded with ten cords of bull pine, cut into four-foot lengths. While this was going on, Nuck Gutterson and I put into The Corposant for a meal and a friendly chat.

The joint was full of rivermen of one calling or other. Brigs, sloops, and scows too jury-rigged to have a proper label all plied the Sacramento, and their crews were all represented. Nuck slurped up a bowl of what the proprietor said was rattlesnake soup.

I stuck to crackers and cheese and struck up a conversation with an old-timer named Leidesdorf. He squinted at me as if sizing me up, but I soon discovered that he squinted all the time. He was a fair-complected man with a spiderweb-patterned nose and an accent that I took to be German until he corrected me and said it was Swiss. "Like Captain Sutter's," he added.

Leidesdorf was referring to the gentleman who founded New Helvetia, as Sacramento was called when it was a lonely fort and trading post. Sutter had not prospered by the gold excitement; too many squatters ran him off his own land. This countryman of Sutter's had a similar tale.

I do not know if like calls to like or not, but out of all the sailors in the place, I had happened on another steamer swab. "Not no more, of course," he said. "I haf a dry goods store here in Sac. Sell denim britches to the miners. But I had a steamboat once."

"What happened?"

Leidesdorf rubbed his balding pate and squinted at his empty tumbler on the counter. I took the hint. "Another glass for my thirsty friend," I called.

"Much obliged," said Leidesdorf after tossing back a slug of abominable gin. "She was called *Sitka* because uff I bought her from the Russians up Alaska way. Thirty-seven feet long and forty tons burden."

I rubbed my mouth to hide a smile. *Sitka* would have fit in the *World's* grand salon, with space left over for the billiard tables. "Go on."

"Eighteen forty-seven. We was the first steamer on dis river." The old man pounded his fist on the bar as if demanding respect of his achievement. "I run her up to New Helvetia, till she sank in a storm." He shook his head sadly at the memory.

"How long were you on the run?"

He wobbled his head again, flashing great, flamboyant side-whiskers like white signal flags. "Three months and my beautiful *Sitka* went to the bottom."

"Beautiful, my aunt Tillie's pig," snorted someone from down the bar. "She was only nine feet on the beam and slow as molasses; a rowboat could beat her in a race.

Six days to come up from Frisco, ain't that the truth, Leidesdorf? An ox team bested her time and the drover stopped and slept every night on the way!"

This sally was greeted with hoots and approving laughter from some in the room, especially from a pair dressed more like miners than sailors. One was a strongly built man wearing a leather jacket. The other was thin, dark haired, and had a scar on his face.

Leidesdorf stuck his nose in his glass and hunched his head between his shoulders. It did not appear that he would add anything more, so I turned to see who had busted in on the conversation.

The man who had spoken was dressed in captain's rig, smartly turned out. His spade beard was black; so were his eyes. And, as it later appeared, so was his heart. "To butt so bluntly into someone else's conference makes you some kind of authority," I said. "But on what? Rudeness? Sarcasm?"

If I had hollered "Fire" I could not have cleared the bar any faster. Even Leidesdorf, who had been at my elbow, disappeared. Just that quick there was no one between devil-face and me. Nuck Gutterson, bless his heart, jumped up to second me, but I waved him back to his chair and his soup.

We met eye-to-eye, this other captain and me, and if we had been flint and steel, we could have burned the place down. He was shorter than me and slighter of build. The fire in his eye showed me the small man's chip on his shoulder. I noted the lack of visible weapons and figured him for a knife wielder; in his shirt collar perhaps.

Also, he was drinking left-handed; an absolutely important thing to note before getting into a shindy. His face was unmarred; a long, straight, almost pointed nose. For someone as on the prod as he seemed to be, that could only mean that he was very good, that he fought dirty, or that he was vain and protected his face; probably all three.

A space of a minute passed with the two of us sizing each other up. The owner of the saloon, no doubt thinking of his priceless nail-keg furniture and even more valuable tangle-leg whiskey, intervened. "Please Cap'n Marrasco, don't kill nobody. He's new here. He didn't know who you was. Don't you nor Wick nor Mister Buck start nothing."

I gathered Wick and Buck were Marrasco's cronies seated together.

Marrasco stiffened as if the plea for peace would push him into fighting. Then, just as he looked like jumping for me, his shoulders relaxed. That change of appearance did not mean I quit watching him, however.

"I'm the boss of this river," he said, thumping his chest. "Ain't that so, Phipps?" he asked the bartender, who nodded vigorously. "Ain't it so?" he then demanded of the crowd. There was a murmur of agreement; half-hearted, I thought.

"And what makes you so?" I hazarded. "Did you win an election, or did you just make yourself king for life?"

Phipps, the bartender, figured the dustup was on for

certain now. He grabbed two bottles of brandy from the shelf and hunkered down behind the counter.

But Marrasco decided to be expansive with his credentials instead of his fists. He gestured broadly toward the glassless windows that confronted The Corposant and waved a regal hand. "There," he said pointing at a tall, white, side-wheel steamer just coming into view. "There's my bona fides. I'm captain of *Goliath*."

I had just met my competition.

The hackles on Captain Marrasco's neck stood up just like a banty rooster's when he found out who I was. A string of profanity such as I had never heard before fairly sulphur-tinged the air. It made me think that he would come for me after all.

Something in my eye, my size, or perhaps the number of witnesses made him draw back. Men of his stripe do not attack without a clear advantage, unless absolutely forced to it. Generally they are backstabbers, or the kind who pay others to do their skullduggery. He continued to reel off oaths until he ran out of steam and just stopped.

Marrasco straightened up after relieving himself of the cargo of blasphemies. Maybe he had shipped the load of curses sometime before and needed to shift his ballast of maledictions or founder with the weight of them. In any case he heaped imprecations on my head and then departed, saying no upstart, thievin', blank-blank was going to best his time or steal his passengers . . .

this matter would be settled on the river. The two cut-throats known as Walter Buck and Clyde Wick went with him.

After his departure, nobody seemed to want to be friendly with me any more. "Come on," I said to Nuck. "Let's get back to the boat." Then to Phipps I said, "What do I owe you for the grub?"

Shaking his head, Phipps said it was on the house. "I don't expect to see you in here again," he added.

"Meaning we aren't wanted?"

"Not at all," he protested. "If you're smart you won't go nowhere Marrasco is. And if you ain't that smart, well—I still won't see you no more."

Pleasant conversation for a pretty summer afternoon. Nuck and I went out of The Corposant to find old Leidesdorf hiding in the willows between the grogshop and the wharf. "I admire you, Mister Maddox," he said. "But you need be warned about Marrasco. He won't never let anybody get crossways uff of him and stay afloat."

"Thanks," I said dryly. "I heard this already. How does he come by such a fearsome reputation?"

Nuck tugged at my sleeve, and muttered, "Rafer, Mister Maddox—"

"Hold on, Nuck," I said. "Let me hear the answer."

"They say he was behind a fire on the *Senator*," Leidesdorf said, "and the explosion that sank the *Freedom*, and maybe he had Captain Oliver thrown overboard and drownded, and . . ." his voice dropped to a rough whisper. "He may be the one who did in my *Sitka*."

Nuck interrupted again by slapping my shoulder "Rafer!"

"What?" I demanded roughly. "What's so all-fired important that it can't wait a minute?"

Pointing toward a thin stream of gray smoke, Nuck asked, "Ain't that our woodpile burning?"

It was indeed. Nuck and I left Leidesdorf in the dust and willows and raced to the wooding yard. My chief concern was that the fire would spread to the *World*.

When we got to the wharf, a heap of about three cords was blazing and the smoke blotted out the sun. The timber boss and his crew had already made a fire-break around the burning pine, and the lack of breeze meant that there was no danger to my ship.

"How did this get started?" I asked the foreman.

He pointed out to me that the fire had commenced in the woodpile closest to a thicket of cottonwoods and elderberry bushes. In other words, someone used the cover of the trees to sneak up unseen and torch the woodpile.

"So it was deliberate. But I don't want to jump to any conclusions," I said. "Is it somebody mad at you or me?"

The timber boss handed me a note, scrawled on half a sheet of foolscap. He said he found it in a bottle back in the thicket. "Don't sell wood to *New World*," it said. "This could have been your home."

The rest of our load of wood was stacked shortly after the fire and we went aboard to ready *New World* for her downstream journey. I posted Nuck back on the smokestack lookout; a position we had not expected to need once on the river but that we had not had time to dismantle.

Nuck asked me what he was to be on the lookout for. That was not a question I could answer, but it made me feel better to have him on watch.

Leaving behind the tents, the sailboats, the fledgling businesses, and the oak trees of Sacramento, the *World* backed away from the dock with 130 miners aboard. These were all gents who had enough in their pokes to want to celebrate, and needed a faster place than Sacramento to spend their money. San Francisco called to them and they were flocking there.

We put in to pick up some more customers at the little settlement known as Freeport. Ahead on the river I could see the stack and the churning water of another steamer. It had already called on Freeport and was shaping downriver.

When I inquired on the dock as to the identity of the other ship, I was told that she was *Goliath*. My second encounter with Marrasco seemed destined to be the same day. His curses rankled when I recalled how I had kept down the notion of thrashing him in favor of a peaceful settlement. Maybe there was a way to keep the peace and still resolve the issue.

Urging Olson to give me a full head of steam, I put the *World* through her paces. I wanted to prove that not only was she the newest and the best; she was fastest too.

Gaining ground on *Goliath*'s stern gave me opportunity to study her through the glass. She was smaller in length than the *World* and shorter as well. Despite those differences, she looked trim and well maintained and worthy of racing against.

Whatever else may have been true about Marrasco, he knew how to run a ship and keep her in form, but *Goliath*'s smaller paddle wheels were a handicap compared to the *World*. Our eight-foot-wide buckets and forty-foot-diameter paddles could move a lot of water, mighty fast.

Along about Merritt Island, we overtook *Goliath*. The river was full of summer runoff from the melting snow of the Sierras and the channel was broad and deep. On Fouratt's chart there were no snags, bars, or hidden obstacles. In other words, it was a perfect place to pass.

I tickled the steam whistle to let Marrasco know I was overtaking him on the port side. Competition might lead to racing, but courtesy was rooted in safety. There was no reason not to have both. As we edged up next to *Goliath*, I allowed a good fifty feet of water between the hulls and another fifty feet separated us from the east bank.

My vantage point in the pilothouse was above Marrasco's helm station. Our weather deck was a full eight feet above *Goliath*'s top deck.

Now I will admit that it was perhaps not wise of me to tip my hat and smile as *World* slid by *Goliath*. It probably would have been better if we had just cruised past in a businesslike way. Marrasco may have taken my friendly gesture for braggadocio.

Thinking back on his reaction, that is what I have to believe.

Instead of following the curve of the bank when it made its next turn to the west, *Goliath* continued straight on as if her rudder were broken. Since we were following the bend but on the outside line, *Goliath*'s drift put her on a collision course for our starboard paddle wheel.

I leaned on the whistle then, of course; gave it all I had to let Marrasco know of the impending collision. At the same time I started chasing more room. Soon the *World* was crowding the tule reeds along the shoreline and churning mud up under her paddles.

Still *Goliath* came on. He meant to ram us on purpose! Marrasco's banner—a crudely drawn giant holding a club in one hand—floated from the jackstaff. It could have been a pennant on the lance of an ancient knight riding to the joust. (I did not have a moment for so literary a thought right then, only later.)

When the bow of the oncoming steamer had closed half the distance that separated us, I laid on the whistle again and almost wrenched the engine room bell off the ceiling by enthusiastically ringing for still more power.

My thinking was that if I could stay clear long enough to avoid being struck on the wheel guard, then *New World*'s tapering stern might slip past unscathed. The *World* shuddered, protesting the extra pressure on her frame.

Gutterson was hollering from his lookout post like a tribe of Red Indians was attacking. Since *Goliath* was about to strike us amidships, I could no longer see her from the wheelhouse. I had to rely on instinct alone. And my instincts told me we were not going to make it.

If the bow of Marrasco's ship struck us in the paddle wheel, it might not sink us, but the damage done would keep us out of business for a month of repairs. That left me only one course of action. I wrenched the wheel hard to port, and hunted grass with the bow.

There was a giant water oak about as big as a house directly in front of us and a clump of tules just upstream of that. I leaned into the turn with all my force and prayed that the *World* would turn inside before busting her nose on the oak tree.

She tried hard, but could have used another six feet of clearance. The gangplank suspended over the bow flailed to kindling. The bow itself scraped a ten-inch-wide swath of bark off that tree trunk and the portside wheel scrabbled on a mud bank, sending *New World* lurching like a drunken sailor. If Baby Moses had been in the bulrushes that day we would have run over him for sure.

Goliath did not hit us, but Nuck told me later we could not have been spared by more than a foot, if that. Marrasco laid on his whistle as he chugged past, and I warrant he had taught that steam pipe to blaspheme. At least it sounded that way to me.

When the stern of *Goliath* passed out of sight around the next bend, I could still hear screeching. I wondered if my ears were damaged some way, or if I was imagining things. Then I remembered that we were carrying passengers.

Our impetuous maneuver into Snodgrass Slough had not done the customers one bit of good. Drinks and drunks both spilled on the deck and several fights started over someone's lap being suddenly occupied by two bearded strangers. The only ones happy about the transaction were those who had been losing at cards; there was no way to prove to whom the scattered chips belonged.

We tried to pole her free, but *New World* remained obstinately fixed on the shore. The only remedy was to lighten ship, and this we accomplished by disembarking the passengers. Since there was now no gangplank or any dock, 130 miners were soon up to their knees in the tule bog.

Olson reversed her and after some more vigorous exercise with twelve-foot-long canes, she floated free. As the *World* idled beside the bank, we added insult to injury by making the passengers wade into waist-deep water to get back aboard.

I assessed the damage. The port wheel had been sanded down an inch; no real harm. The gangplank was a total loss of course, but could be replaced in a couple days, and the *World* was still operable. Greater injury had been done to our unformed reputation: A hundred miners said that if that was how we were going to run a steamboat, they'd rather ride a mule.

The other thirty promised that they would return, but only on one condition: They insisted that I turn *Goliath* into matchsticks at the earliest opportunity. It seemed the feud was on.

CHAPTER 7

When we arrived back in Frisco, *Goliath* was moored up only two warves away, chuffing little easy knots of steam as if to say to the *World*, What kept you? Resisting the impulse to give my fist a close acquaintance with Marrasco's nose, I bypassed the pleasure and went to report in. Wakeman's new office was on the upper side of Montgomery, right where Washington bottomed out. He had secured space in the Archer Mercantile establishment.

The Archer building looked imposing from a hundred yards away; so did the entire block in fact. The columned arcades that fronted the three-story structures gave an air of respectability and permanence to the endeavors. From twenty-five yards away the onlooker's confidence wavered some, and upon close inspection, the truth was made manifest. Like an aging harridan painted and bejeweled to keep up appearances, the Archer building was all lath and canvas, pretending to look like stone and masonry. In short, it was a fraud. The fluted pillars proved to be ship masts appropriated from derelicts in the harbor, and the upper stories were a sham.

Inside the firm were mining implements that were real enough and prices that while appearing impossibly high were nevertheless indisputable. A shovel worth fifty cents back in the States was five dollars—gold. Luxury items like shirts were even more extravagantly priced.

In a corner, behind a brass cashier's cage, was a desk. A sign on the grill read NEW WORLD TRANSPORTA-TION COMPANY—FREIGHT AND PASSENGERS FOR SACRAMENTO. "So, Captain Maddox," Wakeman greeted me, "a successful first voyage. How many passengers on the return?"

I told him, then launched into a recital about Marrasco's boasting and his attempt to ram us. Wakeman's neck turned red and he clenched and unclenched his fists. It was clear that he was in the grip of powerful emotions, as incensed as I was at the lack of chivalry on the river; infuriated by a complete breakdown in the camaraderie shared by sailors.

My satisfaction was short-lived. "And you say you saw him turn toward you?" I allowed that I had. "And you did not fire a shot into his pilothouse, even though you have the height on him? Neptune's beard, man! The *World* could climb over the top of *Goliath* and grind her to powder. How could you let him best you that way and get off scot-free? Didn't you at least make up the time on the next stretch? Why isn't his boat wrapped around a cottonwood at this very minute?"

Explaining about our navigation of Snodgrass Slough did not improve matters any. "You let him damage company property, inconvenience our passengers, and disrupt our schedule without any consequences?" Wakeman fairly shouted at me.

"What did you have in mind?" I asked dryly. "It seems to me that you are more upset with me than you are with Marrasco."

It did not surprise me that he agreed with that statement. "River traffic is rough-and-tumble out here," Wakeman lectured. "You challenged the man, made to pass him, and yet made no allowance for his response? Rafer, I'm very disappointed. All you would have needed to do was fire a round or two into the wheelhouse and he would have kept his distance. This whole business is as much your fault as it is his."

It was on the tip of my tongue to tell him exactly what I thought of conducting business out west, if that was the way of it. I did not speak though, because I had to admit that there was more than a grain of truth to what he said; not about shooting into the helm station, but about me having provoked the incident. Anyway, once again it had been proved that I had much to learn about California. Getting discharged from my first command after my first voyage did not seem reasonable either. I held my peace.

"Enough of that now," Wakeman allowed graciously. "I'm sure you won't let it happen again. I want you to meet our latest business associate. This is Gam Gillis. He's our new agent."

The gentleman Wakeman indicated was a study in contradictions. He wore his hair long like a miner newly down from the diggings, but was clean shaven. His hat was raked fore-and-aft, as if inviting a fight, but there was a merry twinkle in his eye. He dressed sailor fashion, in dungarees and neckerchief, but his belly was plump and his hands were soft. As I soon learned, his greatest stock-in-trade was gab, which squared with his nickname, *gam* being the seagoing word for a palaver.

"What do you think of Rafer's encounter with *Goliath?*" Wakeman asked Gillis when we had completed our greetings.

"It's a bad business," Gillis said with a smile. His manner continued the contradictions begun by his looks. Then he explained. "Can't have the *World* getting the reputation for being an easy target. Just think how Marrasco could spread the word that Maddox here was afraid; be terrible for business. Then not overhauling *Goliath* on the river . . . why Marrasco could say that Maddox was scared of too much steam pressure that the *World* was unsafe."

"That'd be a lie! I snorted.

Gillis appeared not to have heard me. "Quickest way to square it all is to get the jump on him. I'll let it be known that . . ." He stopped and the flicker of humor in his face disappeared for a moment, only to resurface an instant later in fuller radiance. "I have it," he exclaimed. "We'll say that during *Goliath*'s wanton attack, three . . . no, make it five . . . five of her passengers were knocked overboard and that Marrasco refused to stop the race to retrieve them. Maddox here lost because *he* stopped to save their lives. That'll do it."

"That'll do it?!" I exploded. "There's not a grain of truth to it—not a speck more than for Marrasco to say that I'm a coward."

"Perfect," Wakeman agreed with Gillis. "Can you get it out today?"

"It'll be the talk of the waterfront in half an hour and in all the papers by tomorrow," Gillis boasted. "Here's one better: Maddox was unable to save all five. Two of them drowned."

"This is insufferable!" I might as well have been all alone in the room for all the effect my protests had.

"'Course, we can't name 'em," Gillis added, sounding a trifle disappointed. "Slander. That might lead to bloodshed." I had a fractional moment of relief that he was coming to his senses. Then Gillis brightened again. "I know! We'll say they were Chinese. Marrasco wouldn't dare say he was libeled over a pair of Celestials. He'd be laughed out of court. This way Marrasco won't have any occasion to call Maddox out."

"Call *me* out!"

"Leave it to me," Gillis announced again. "Be seeing you gentlemen later."

The departure of our new business associate left me speechless and staring for a time. Eventually I recovered enough to inquire of Wakeman, "Where did you get him?"

"Worth his weight in gold dust," Wakeman crowed. "Best there is. Drums up business for *New World* while stoving in the chances of the others."

"I believe I understand what an agent does," I commented with an edge of sarcasm. "I wanted to know where you found him."

"Hired him away from Marrasco," was the reply.

The fact that Jamie O'Reilly was the only woman to arrive in San Francisco aboard the *New World* should have served as warning to her. In 1850, the year of the Golden Emigration, the San Francisco newspapers reported the male population of the city at 35,333. There were only 1,248 women. From an overland count made at Fort Laramie, an additional 39,560 men were headed west. Only 2,421 women and 604 children came with them.

Most of the females remained in San Francisco or Sacramento City. There were only a literal handful in the hills and gold camps. Those single women who traveled the back trails did so in order to sell body and soul in a lucrative business. Prostitutes were counted among the wealthy of those in the West.

Such facts as these made the presence of a respectable woman like Mrs. O'Reilly traveling in the company of a priest a cause for astonishment and celebration. In Hangtown, a small collection of Catholics came for confession and attended their first Mass in two months. At sight of the beautiful Mrs. O'Reilly they crossed themselves and genuflected. Within hours, miners of every religious persuasion or no religion at all left their claims and flocked to see her. She and the Mexican drover cooked a simple meal of bacon, beans, and cornbread for the priest's small congregation. All such efforts were halted as hundreds of men arrived bearing every type of game and provisions. A French trapper and his buckskin-clad Scottish partner skinned six deer, and a feast of venison was prepared in her honor. This was accompanied by everything from fried trout to quail-egg omelettes prepared with wild mushrooms and onions. Jamie's beans and bacon were fed to the Indians, who peered out from the brush in curiosity at the hubbub.

I heard of this much after the event and had to smile at the fact that I had predicted Mrs. O'Reilly would convince the miners that she was the Virgin Mary come down from heaven. The effect on the men could not have been greater if that had been true. They worshiped her, although it is now my firm belief she would have been ill-treated if she had not been in the company of Father Patrick.

As for Jamie, she could think of nothing but finding Danny O'Reilly. She believed that if her husband was anywhere within a hundred miles he would hear that she had come. Then he would find his way to her. With this hope she searched each face and questioned every stranger.

"His name is Daniel. Danny we call him. Danny O'Reilly. He is fair of complexion and slight of build. His hair is tawny colored and his eyes blue."

A few recollected seeing a young, scrawny Irishman called Danny. But Danny was a common name. In the Sierra, surnames were seldom used. There were several thousand micks working placer claims. Blue eyes and yellow-brown hair? Could be ten thousand like that. Who could say if this Dan or that was the one she was looking for?

The priest posted guards around the grounds of the meeting place. Guns were gathered and whiskey was forbidden. After the meal Father Patrick preached the parable of the prodigal son to the mobs of backsliders and unsaved who came to see Mrs. O'Reilly. In his homily, the errant son described by the good priest came home not just to a loving father, but to the arms of grieving mother, sister, and innocent sweetheart. There was not a dry eye in the house by the time he finished.

After the services a penitent young man spoke to the priest in a trembling voice. "Got closer to a decent female this evening than I have been in six months. Came near to fainting. Reminded me of a lot of good things I near forsook out here. I left home innocent and now I done most every sin there is, except the ones I ain't heard of yet. I'm the true prodigal in need of forgiveness, Padre, and that's a fact."

According to the strategy of Father Patrick, the meeting had been a great success. Mrs. O'Reilly, however, was left with her arms still empty. There was not one man among the thousand who offered her any hope at all.

⟨▷◆◁⟩

The day following my encounter with *Goliath* and her master was the Sabbath. *New World*, having proved her soundness for the river trade (as well as having survived her first battle) was docked to begin repair of the damage to her gangplank and for sundry adjustments.

Marrasco drove his boat as he did his crew—hard and without rest. He expected her to be ready to sail every day at ten in the morning, even if all night had been spent in seeing to mechanical needs. He even ran night passages, as demand warranted. Since *Goliath* did not sit idle on Sunday, but went back to Sacramento she was upriver when the *World* was down and vice versa. The schedules of the two boats did not mesh again until a whole week had passed.

Operating on differing calendars did not mean we two captains did not see each other, of course. Once a day we passed rail to rail.

On our first meeting after the race, Marrasco held to the center of the channel as if he believed that I was truly frightened of him. As the vessels closed to within two hundred yards of each other, his confidence wavered when confronted by the *World*'s broad bow and superior size. With time to spare he spun the wheel hard over and crowded the far bank, leaving ample room for the ships to pass unscathed.

Tooting his whistle fiercely and shaking his fist, Marrasco showed his anger and his derision, but he made no hostile move. Possibly this was because I stoically faced forward as if he did not even exist, so as not to provoke him. More likely his inaction was a result of Gutterson's perch on the stack with a .50-caliber Sharps.

We also passed other river traffic. The slender and swift *Antelope* made regular runs, as did Captain Vogel in the *Senator*. None of these encounters resulted in anything like our first competition with *Goliath*.

The second Monday after the rivalry was born, *Goliath* and *World* were again on the same timetable. We backed down from the wharf at precisely ten in the morning. The August passage was jammed with prospective miners, intent on reaching the diggings in time to make their piles before winter closed down the Sierras.

The decks were packed with the remnants of the Tower of Babel. The sugarloaf-shaped hats of Chilean adventurers vied for a place at the rail with the brimless kepis of the French. Silver-concho embellished pantaloons crowded alongside fringed buckskin leggings. Foreigners were plentiful.

Americans of all stripes were likewise represented. Some were well dressed and well spoken; most were clad in sturdy denim, floppy slouch hats, and beards, and punctuated their conversations with discharges of chewing tobacco.

The Chinese were present, but were not seen on the boat. Wakeman decreed (following the lead of other captains in this regard) that the Celestials should not be allowed to mix with the other races. Consequently, Orientals traveling on the steamers were required to stay in the forward cargo hold, enduring the cramped space like so many cattle. For this "privilege" they were charged the same rates of passage as everyone else. While raucous drinking, gambling, and dining were going on in salon and main cabin, the belowdecks compartment stifled in the ninety-degree weather, water buckets being the only allowance for the journey.

New World was filled to capacity for the trip. The competition among the steamers was already benefiting the passengers. Rates were falling. A ticket to Sacramento dropped five dollars. It seemed that Agent Gillis had his work cut out for him.

Shaking off whatever bad press my handling of the race may have occasioned, *New World* being both fast and opulent attracted attention. Wakeman authorized Elijah to spend lavishly in the preparation of meals; beefsteak was customary and even oysters were common fare. The *World*'s red plush cushions and marble counters attracted the rich, those who fancied becoming rich, and those who intended to feast on the frailties of the recently enriched.

We took on additional freight at a village known as New York of the Pacific. *Goliath* had already called there and was still ahead of us on the river. As the *World* entered the bend just below Grand Island, Gutterson sang out, "Smoke ahead! 'Nuther boat ahead of *Goliath*."

"Bound down or up?" I called.

"Up," was the reply.

"Can you make her out?"

"She's narrow. Could be *Antelope* . . . no, I only see two pennants."

Every boat had some distinguishing features that helped a lookout discern identities over long distances. In the case of the *World* it was sheer size, but there were other subtleties as well. *Goliath*, for example, had two flagpoles, one at her bow and one amidships, back of her stack. *Antelope*, given to showy displays, had four pennant masts equally spaced down her hull.

"Is her pilothouse higher than her wheel guards?" I yelled up.

There was a pause while Nuck studied the other ship's outline. "Yep," he agreed. "Must be the *Wheeler*."

So it proved. Fouratt's magic trick of pulling a

steamship out of a sunken bark had been completed. *Wheeler*, her paddles reinstalled and her superstructure reassembled, was cruising upriver at a respectable ten knots.

"That'll drive Marrasco crazy," I called. "He thinks there's too much competition now."

From the cloud of black smoke that obscured the bright blue sky it appeared that Marrasco was stoking the furnace, intending to make a race of it. Just as evident was the fact that Fouratt was not going to surrender easily. *Wheeler*'s stack also belched smoke and Fouratt steered for midchannel, denying Marrasco the opportunity to pass.

When we drew abreast of Hogback Slough, the two boats ahead were passing the Ryer Island ferry. Marrasco was crowding the stern of Fouratt's boat. *Goliath* had a full head of steam up and was showing that she did possess a turn of speed greater than *Wheeler* could match.

Races are not decided solely by speed, however. In Captain Fouratt, Marrasco had met his equal in determination and stubbornness. From our position astern as spectators, the contest was a matter of Fouratt hanging on to his lead by any means possible.

Goliath swept up hard on *Wheeler*'s starboard side. The next bend ahead was to the right, so Marrasco had positioned his boat to lunge ahead if Fouratt swung wide on the curve.

With a memory like Fouratt's, it was unlikely he would fall prey to such a misjudgment, nor did he. He pushed the *Wheeler* so hard toward the eastern bank that

Goliath almost lost her bow from sticking it where it did not belong.

Though there was water enough for three steamers to run abreast, Fouratt was making *Wheeler* behave like an enraged water snake. The ship was twisting and weaving so as to thwart any possible opening.

From a quarter mile behind I saw Marrasco's temper boil over. Judging his state of mind was easy when *Goliath* charged straight ahead into *Wheeler*'s stern just as the two boats entered the reach below Sutter's Island.

Gutterson sang out, "He's gonna ram!" and in the next second, *Goliath*'s bow collided with *Wheeler* just aft of the starboard paddles. Since Captain Fouratt was already halfway into his turn, the force of the blow pushed the *Wheeler* broadside across *Goliath*'s bow. The two steam whistles bellowed like the battle cries of sparring elephants.

Fouratt's ship was propelled bodily upstream as if she were a bit of floating debris. Pivoting on the point of impact, *Wheeler* spun sharply to starboard, ending up facing downstream as *Goliath* drew apart, victorious for the moment.

A renewed burst of black smoke from *Wheeler*'s stack told me that Fouratt had not given up. As we idled up below the scene in order to keep from harm's way, I watched Fouratt twist his vessel sharply around once more and take off in pursuit.

Wheeler was smaller than either *Goliath* or the *New World*, but that fact alone did not signal that she was not speedy. Her paddle wheels churned the water of the

Sacramento to a white foam in her eagerness to even the score. I put down what happened next to the intensity of the struggle. Enos Fouratt was too salty a sailor to make such an error unless driven blind by rage.

To those who know how to read it, the river's surface is full of signals, warnings, and suggestions. A particular ripple suggests shoal water, a floating log portends a rise, a white streak bordered by blue bands is a sandbar, and so forth. To the uninitiated, the river's features are pretty or nondescript according to the amount of poetry in the viewer's soul. A passenger sees the winding ribbon of water as a highway, but of insignificance compared to the boat.

But a river pilot would never speak in disparaging terms of the waterways. Besides being the lifeblood of his trade, the river speaks to him, sharing secret wisdom and counsel.

So it can only be concluded that massive inattention caused Captain Fouratt to drive *Wheeler* onto the snag. From a full three hundred yards away, Nuck Gutterson remarked the diagonal slash on the water that revealed the presence of a partially submerged tree trunk. "Snag ahead!" he yelled.

"Ohhh!" Scrimshaw screeched, in mimic of Gutterson's worried cry.

By then it was already too late for Fouratt to avoid it. The *Wheeler* ran the spike of the snag directly into her hull on the starboard side forward. Like a cavalry horse charging into an earthwork protected by sharpened stakes, *Wheeler* was impaled. Before Fouratt could react, the churning wheels drove the boat upon the snag, ripping open a gash in the forward hold. *Wheeler* tried to climb over the obstruction, but was unsuccessful. The hull bucked and plunged in an unsuccessful frenzy to free herself.

I signaled for Olson to give me speed and we drew up alongside the stricken steamer. The *Wheeler* was down by the bow. Her hull was raked to a steep angle as more of the bow end of the boat sank, until it reached bottom and perched there. Passengers and crew tumbled down the inclined decks, splashing and floundering.

The hatch of the cargo space burst upward. Dozens of Chinese struggled to get free of the wash. Their long blue cotton coats were sodden and heavy, threatening to pull them under. I saw several hauled to safety by the topknots of their pigtails; a deadly insult at any other time, the circumstances warranted it to save lives.

"Ahoy, Captain Fouratt," I yelled through my hailing trumpet. "I'll lay by and lend a hand." Fouratt waved to acknowledge our presence, but was too busy to reply. His dilemma was that he wanted to set the *Wheeler* back on her engines, but could not do so because of the passengers in the water near the wheels. Many of them climbed over the railings to the *World* as we warped up alongside.

Two of Fouratt's deckhands, Kanakas by the look of their deep brown skin, scrambled over into the water beside the snag. They carried a crosscut saw and a pair of hand axes and set to work loosing *Wheeler* from her torment.

Other passengers transferred to our decks. Fouratt himself came across, the stubby pipe still clamped in his teeth. "How bad is it?" I asked.

Clenching his fists in anger and frustration Fouratt said, "Forward hold is full of water. If we cut the snag free I can drive her up on the bar till we make repairs. Can you take all my passengers?"

"That we can," I said. "Any casualties?"

"Only forward," he said grimly. "Chinese in the hold. Two of them drowned. I'll kill that Marrasco." Saying nothing, I showed my concern with my eyes alone. "I know what you're thinking," he resumed with a grunt. "Marrasco will claim the brush was accidental. *Wheeler* hit the snag after, so the fault there is all mine." He looked me in the face and said quietly, "The reckoning will be paid in full, one of these days."

Of the sincerity of his words I had no doubt. For the time, though, all that remained of *Goliath* was a faint smudge of smoke on the horizon. She had neither turned back nor stopped to help.

Such was the lawless condition of the West in those days that some crimes were harshly suppressed while others were winked at. Horse-stealing and claim-jumping might result in a date with Judge Lynch, but killing an Indian or a Chinaman was not punishable by anything stronger than disapproval, if that. Marrasco's determination to possess unchallenged supremacy on the river had led to property damage and loss of life, but there was no force to bring him to justice. Indeed, much of the society there admired strength above all other qualities.

It is wrong to think that there was no faith or morality out west. Men are men, wherever they are. Those disposed to evil will find a way to practice it, in any circumstance. Those with a genuine relationship with their Creator will experience challenges to faith, but won't part with it. What was true of the West was this: A lack of codified law meant that wickedness flourished more openly than back in the States.

When we reached Sacramento I had formulated a plan. It seemed to me that the only way to deal with Marrasco was to beat him at his own game. If he could be shut down in a race, it might shut him up, at least for a while.

I caught up with him in The Corposant. He was at the bar, boasting of his latest exploit. His spade beard was wagging and the heads of the rough characters around him were nodding in agreement. "Left him holed and sinking," he bragged.

"Nobody can match *Goliath*," the skinny black-haired Wick agreed. "Nobody!"

Marrasco had not seen me enter. Grabbing him by the shoulder, I spun him around. His left hand went to his shirt collar, confirming my thought as to where he hid a blade. I caught his left wrist in my own, yanking it behind his head and holding it there. "Pretty scurvy trick," I said without preamble. "*Goliath* hits the *Wheeler*, then runs away from a stricken vessel without offering assistance. Back east the port authority would pull a pilot's ticket for less."

"Let go of me!" he spat. He jerked his head forward, calling some of his cutthroat crew to help him. I countered by a nod of my own, which brought Gutterson to my left side with an ax handle in plain view facing Wick. Olson stood on my right thumping a two-foot-long steel wrench into his palm and staring down Walter Buck. The patrons of the saloon froze in place. It was obvious to all that the first false move would lead to a broken head. "That brush was an accident," Marrasco asserted. "It's not my fault if Fouratt is old and blind. He had plenty of water to avoid that snag!"

"Maybe so," I allowed. "But for you to know that means you saw the collision, and you made no move to assist."

"My first duty is to my own ship and passengers," the devil-faced captain whined.

"You are lower than a snake's belly, Marrasco, and you are a loser besides. In a fair race you couldn't beat a rowboat."

His swarthy face radiating hatred for my words, he spat at me, "Beat you already, didn't I? Care to try again?"

This was of course exactly the reaction I intended to provoke. "You're on. In two weeks, when we are next on the same run, *New World* challenges *Goliath* to a race. Loser gives up any claim to being fastest on the river."

CHAPTER 8

It would be wrong to say that the two weeks that intervened before the race were uneventful. I had another set-to with Ned Wakeman. He criticized me for stopping to help Fouratt; said I should have sent help back rather than inconveniencing our own passengers. He also said I should have collected at least half fares from the rescued men, or made Fouratt fork over what he had collected. I could hardly bring myself to speak, I was so angry with him. Then of all people, who should speak up on my behalf but Agent Gillis.

Gillis said, "Leave him be, Captain Wakeman. It's fine press for the *World* to do a good turn. Besides, it was purely a piece of inspiration for Maddox here to challenge Marrasco to a race. If . . ." he said to me with a questioning tone, "if you're sure you can win."

"Of course I'm sure," I said. "The *World* is the better boat. I'll stake my position on it."

"Now there's a headline." Gillis pounced. "'Maddox Vows to Quit the River If *New World* Loses Race.' Why

we'll be able to sell tickets at premium prices to partici-
pants!"

"Look," I said, "the point is to get Marrasco to back
off. Not to sell tickets."

But Gillis had the bit in his teeth and was running
away with the story he could pitch to the *Alta Californian* and the *Sacramento Independent*. "Mayhap we can
get each of the newspapers to back a boat; stimulate the
rivalry, you see."

Wakeman liked the idea. "But won't that mean one
of the two will be bad-mouthing us? Let's get the *Alta*
and the *Independent* to both back us. Let Marrasco out-
bid us for their support if he can."

Regardless of what I thought of Gillis and his ways,
he was keeping the *World* well supplied with fare-paying
passengers. Every trip upriver was packed to the rails
with miners. And if the trip downstream was lighter for
people, it was heavier for cargo—produce for the growing settlement of San Francisco.

A few days more passed. Nights I slept aboard the
World, taking turnabout with Nuck in patrolling the
deck. I could scarcely wait for race day, feeling like something would be settled thereby.

It was the morning of another upriver voyage when I
heard an uproar out on the wharf. I roused myself from
my cabin in the texas and went on deck to see to it.

On the pier, just at the *World*'s bow, Gam Gillis was
haranguing a bearded crew of potential customers. In full
voice he was extolling the merits of our boat over all the

others. "Finest liquor," I heard him say. "Choicest vittles. Greatest speed, excellent safety, plushest surroundings."

Turning to reenter my cabin I heard him say, "You don't want to take passage on *Wheeler*. She isn't seaworthy. No sir! You heard about the snag? Fouratt was drunk again. Nearly killed fifty people. Did kill some Chinese. Do you want to take a chance like that with your necks? No, sir. Not anyone with brains. Who cares if you reserved space on that tub? Plenty of room on the *World*. Come on aboard."

That was when I noticed the other man in the bowler hat and the high, stiff-collared shirt. He was screeching as loud or louder than Gillis. He was Barnes, the agent for the *Wheeler*. "Don't believe his lies," the derby-hatted Barnes yelled. "The *World* is practicing for a race, throwing caution to the winds. Does that sound like excellent safety to you?"

Of the two, Gillis was the more persuasive. The potential passengers had indeed heard of the incident upriver. It was easy to make them believe that Fouratt and liquor had led to the accident. "Put your lives in the hands of a juiced-up old fool like Fouratt?" Gillis pushed his advantage. "Why take that chance?"

At that juncture Barnes leaped for Gillis. The bowler hat skittered off toward the bay and the shindy was on. A regular dustup was in progress, with Gillis smacking Barnes in the nose just before Barnes's hands closed around his throat. It seemed that the honor of the boats and the personal veracity of the agents could only be settled by mortal combat.

Stepping into the pilothouse, I took up the Sharps propped there from Gutterson's guard duties. Apologizing to Scrimshaw for the noise I was about to make, back out on deck I went. The fight was still on, so I fired a round into the water. The roar of the Sharps rolled over the crowd. All of them dived for cover behind herring barrels and piles of canvas. Like a conjuring trick, the arena was suddenly vacant except for the two combatants, who were locked with Gillis's thumb in Barnes's eye and Barnes's teeth on Gillis's earlobe. "Belay that!" I yelled in my most commanding voice. "Leave off, Mister Gillis!"

Dusting himself off and wiping the blood trickling down his cheek from his wounded ear, Gillis said plaintively, "He started it, Captain Maddox."

"I overheard the conversation," I said. "Gentlemen," I addressed the prospectors. "Captain Fouratt was not drunk and the *Wheeler* is a fine ship. You do not need to be afraid to book passage on her."

That broke up the mob. Barnes looked surprised and Gillis gave me the dirtiest look ever. My little speech had not made him mend his ways, however. When last seen he had gathered another group of voyagers around him to address. Agenting had come to mean stealing the clients of other steamers. There was no law against that either.

Portsmouth Square was one area of San Francisco that in 1850 was recognizable from one month to the next. No matter how many times the place burned down, the inhabitants felt the need to rebuild that particular space to almost identical dimensions. It had become a sort of touchstone for the fledgling city.

It was in Portsmouth Square that I encountered Wakeman just after my set-to with Agent Gillis. It was in my mind to give him my view of Gillis's activities. I did not intend to get Gillis fired, but I did think Wakeman could cool him out some.

In any case, it was in front of an old Spanish adobe belonging to the former alcaldes of San Francisco that my course brought me squarely into Wakeman. He was wearing a tight-fitting rig of the new style—stovepipe trouser legs, a short jacket, and a scowl like the blackest squall ever seen off the California coast.

"Hello, Ned," I said amiably, reasoning that his fuming countenance might be due to the foul-smelling cigar he was holding. "You know, Gillis and me—"

I got no farther in my recital because Wakeman took over the helm at that point and refused to relinquish it. "Aha!" he said forcefully, like firing a round across my bow. "Gillis, indeed!"

"Yes," I said. "Gillis was—"

"You turncoat mutineer!" he snapped. "If I had another pilot I ought to break you right now. Where do you get off interfering with *New World*'s agent in the performance of his duties? Sending passengers to another boat? Speaking up for another steamer line?"

"Whoa," I said, trying to get ahead-full reduced to a

slower pace. "Gillis was telling lies about Enos Fouratt. All I did was separate him from . . ."

"You mind your own business," Wakeman ordered, throwing down the Havana Perfecto and stomping on the butt. His mood and actions indicated that he wished it were my head under his heel. "You could have just let it be. Gillis can take care of himself. But no! You not only interfered, you busted in on the wrong side!"

"See here, Ned!"

"Captain Wakeman to you," he insisted. "You're on a short reach and headed straight for the shoals. Get your thinking straightened out, Maddox. Get on board with my plans for my steamship line."

"Your line?" I queried. "What would Mister Brown say about the way you and Gillis conduct his affairs?"

"Brown has nothing to say in the matter. *New World* is wholly my concern, and don't you forget it!" he said seriously, recovering his aplomb by straightening his jacket and withdrawing another cigar from the breast pocket. "Maddox, you can redeem yourself and your future with this concern if you win the race. But win it you must and convincingly too. There must be no half-measures; no room for remaining skepticism. The *World* must be the undisputed queen of the river. Now, you'll have to excuse me. I'm meeting some other businessmen to discuss statehood."

To say that Wakeman's diatribe had left me reeling would be to compare a hurricane to a little blow of wind. I had imagined that like owner Brown, Wakeman would also disapprove of underhanded tactics. Apparently I was wrong.

Father Patrick, Jamie, and the Mexican cook finally reached the outskirts of Nevada City. Their long trek from the Sacramento Valley had taken them past hundreds of miners laboring in the cold, snow-fed waters of the western Sierra. At every campsite the priest inquired after Danny O'Reilly while Jamie and the Mexican remained at a distance. In spite of this precaution, a Tennessean caught sight of Mrs. O'Reilly. He whooped three times, sending the announcement that a momentous event was at hand. Though no one had any further word of Jamie's lost man, there were suddenly three hundred fellows who volunteered to find him for her. When, at last, the trio entered Nevada City in the late afternoon, a herd of miners trooped after them.

Nevada City was a collection of ramshackle huts and canvas lean-tos set among the stunted digger pines. Jamie could not help but look and wonder where Danny had camped during his stay here. His last letter had been clearly addressed Nevada City. She had imagined him in a town of brick and wood; shingled roofs, paved roads, and boardwalks. There was hardly anything here to deserve the title "City." A few real buildings were being raised. Among the new construction was a half-finished two-story structure that was intended to become a saloon. This was owned by the duly elected mayor, a former Mississippi gambler by the name of North who had gone west after killing a senator's son in a duel.

At the first sight of Jamie, the hammering ceased. A loud cry was raised, "WOMAN IN THE CAMP!" This usually meant that a prostitute had arrived.

Workers leaped from the scaffolding and clambered through the mud to see Jamie. There was some grumbling upon observation that the female was in the company of a brown-robed padre. The mayor, sensing the opportunity for publicity, offered his half-completed saloon as shelter for the woman and the priest and their helper.

Mayor North doffed his hat and said, "It is not a palace, as a woman of such quality deserves, but it is the only place with a wood plank floor between here and Sacramento." The offer was gratefully accepted on behalf of Jamie, who remained silent and with her eyes downcast as was fitting.

A cheer rose up from the crowd. A lady of quality would be spending the night in Nevada City! From somewhere in the back of the crowd came the shout, "Let's have a wingding! Let the golden lady reign as queen tomorrow!" Plans for a celebration to rival Independence Day were suddenly in the works.

The suggestion was seconded by hurrahs and gunshots. The joy of the crowd seemed near to disintegrating into a riot. Individual fistfights broke out when disagreements arose as to whether Mrs. O'Reilly was or was not the most beautiful woman ever yet seen on the face of the earth and whether she alone was entitled to the title of Golden Lady. It seemed the crown had been promised to a woman of ill-repute who often dropped into Nevada City on her regular route. After all, did not the harlot better represent the spirit of California than a respectable woman?

The mayor tried to quiet the spirits of the men, but was drowned out by boos and handfuls of mud. On the fringe of the dispute a lean-to was knocked down. A mule kicked over a barrel of whiskey. This began yet another brawl between the owner of the animal and the owner of the liquor.

Jamie remarked to the mayor, "I have seen donny-brooks before, but usually from drinking the whiskey, not spilling it."

The mayor replied, "Whiskey is mother's milk here, madam. And you can see how these gents value all things related to motherhood." His gaze swept appreciatively over her figure.

She replied, "Your citizens have an odd way of showing appreciation."

"This is peaceable compared to what will come of tomorrow's celebration. The boys get happy and somebody always gets killed from it."

It was then that Father Patrick climbed onto a wagon bed and bowed his head as if to pray. No one shot him for it in spite of the fact that this act was a bucket of cold water on a party that was only just getting wound up. When shouts fell away and peace was restored Father Patrick declined the queenship on Jamie's behalf. "It would not be fitting for Mrs. O'Reilly to participate in such a celebration what with her husband missing and his fate unknown to her."

Relieved, Jamie whispered her gratitude to the priest. The mayor then announced to all, "In honor of Mrs. O'Reilly, I shall christen my glorious new establishment, the Golden Lady." He turned to her with a smile "How is that for showing appreciation?"

Jamie conceded that it was fine, but she would rather have her husband. Then the young wife stood upon the newly arrived piano and pleaded for anyone with news of her husband to come forward. No one budged, although it seemed to Jamie that there was a stirring among a half dozen rough-looking fellows near the back of the mob. A few seconds passed before a black-bearded, long-shanked man in a slouch hat broke from the group, grabbed his horse, and rode out of town. This gave Jamie a moment of hope. Was the rider taking word to Danny in some far-off ravine?

She called, "Last word I had of my husband was in late '49. He was here among you at Nevada City."

A blond-bearded man replied, "Most everybody that was here then is long gone now. We're what you might call the second shift."

Mayor North confirmed this information. "The first placer claims played out six months ago. The forty-niners drifted on. These gents came after."

"But . . . drifted on? Where?" she pleaded.

The mayor stroked his close-trimmed beard. "Any one of a thousand places, I fear. There's a new tent city sprung up in every ravine where even a hint of color is spotted in the creekbed. Some have gone up north. Others are working claims three hundred miles south of here. Smart ones have gone into selling dry goods or herding Spanish cattle. Hard to say where that man of yours has got to."

Jamie's hope evaporated. Danny had undoubtably left the area when the first claims had played out. Where, in all the vast territory of California, was she to look for him? What if he had sent another letter, telling her where he was? What if he had returned to find her gone? What a fool she had been to come to California.

Downcast, she stepped back and turned away.

Father Patrick took over the makeshift podium. Smiling cheerfully, he announced, "Rarely have I laid eyes on a more pathetic pack of wolves and cutthroats than you. I'll be available immediately for confession. It's plain from the looks of you, you're in need." He rubbed his hands together eagerly like a man ready to eat a hearty meal. "After we get your sins straightened out—this may take a bit longer than usual—Mass will be held behind the Golden Lady." His declaration caused an uneasy rustling. He offered up a blessing on behalf of Nevada City. The riot was thwarted and the crowd dispersed.

Jamie carried her meager belongings into the roofless saloon and made herself a small room out of blankets strung from ropes. This was the first wooden floor she had walked on since leaving San Francisco. Dry planks beneath her seemed a great luxury. She sank down on her bedroll in exhaustion and closed her eyes for a moment. Falling instantly into a deep sleep, she dreamed of Danny and Ireland and the hunger that had driven them from the shores of their homeland. The gaunt faces of her mother and sisters were vivid before her. Bowls on the table were empty. The peat fire had gone out. It was cold and dark. Then the silhouette of Danny appeared in the doorway of the cottage. She tried to see his face but there was not light enough. Far away, his voice spoke her name and told her about a golden land where there was no hunger and where a man could till his own acres and raise his children without fear.

"Where is this place?" she asked him.

"On the far side of the wide, wide waters, my love. 'Tis where I've gone to, Jamie. I'll see you there." With that, he vanished.

"Danny!" she cried from her dream. "Where are you? Where have you gone? I've come so far to find you. Where have you gone?"

There was no reply. She looked long at the empty bowls on the scarred old table and the familiar faces of her family receded into a dark mist.

Jamie did not know how long she slept. The sound of footsteps awakened her. She sat up. A pair of mud-encrusted hobnailed boots were visible at the hem of the blanket partition.

"Danny?" she cried. "Is that you, Danny?" Jumping to her feet, she threw back the curtain. The pained face of the dark-bearded rider was before her.

"What? . . . Do you know where he is, sir?" She blurted, ashamed of her show of emotion.

The dark man's mouth opened slowly then closed

again. He groaned, as though he wanted to speak but could not. Placing his fingers to his lips, he moaned again, opened his mouth and showed Jamie that he had no tongue.

She flinched and stared at him, finally managing to say, "I am sorry. Father Patrick is behind the saloon. If you wish to see him—"

The man shook his head in vigorous disagreement. He held up his hand as if to tell her she should not be afraid of him. But she was frightened all the same. Pushing past her, he grasped her wrist. He pulled the partition closed and stood panting in front of her.

"Get out!" she spat. "Or I'll scream and you will not escape alive!"

Holding a finger to his lips he looked at her with pleading eyes. Then he reached into the pocket of his canvas vest and pulled out a long, rumpled, brown envelope; sealed by a thick drop of bloodred wax; imprinted by a thumb.

In spite of the weak and spidery scrawl, the handwriting was still as familiar to Jamie as Danny's voice. "From Danny?" she whispered, taking the letter from the dark man. But it was not addressed to her. Danny's words forbade her to open it. The warning confirmed her worst fears:

Upon peril of the soul of he who bears this letter:

Seal to be broken, contents read only by a priest of the holy Catholic Church.

Concerning the last confession of Daniel Robert O'Reilly:

Jamie felt the color drain from her face. The room began to spin. She sank to her knees and held the envelope to her heart. "Ah, no!" she choked. "Daniel O'Reilly! Have you left me so entirely alone then?"

She closed her eyes and waited until the rush of blood stopped pounding in her ears. When she finally looked up, the dark messenger had gone.

Groping for the wall, she managed to stand, swaying for a moment. Her tears surprised her. She had not known she was crying. Everything seemed distant. Numbness engulfed her. Wiping her eyes with the back of her hand she walked deliberately out of the skeleton of the saloon into the soft evening light.

Father Patrick was preparing the Communion table on the back of a wagon. The Mexican was stirring a cauldron of beans.

The priest glanced up. His easy grin vanished. "What is it, girl?" Father Patrick rushed to her side.

"A letter . . . from my husband." She clung to him. "It is addressed . . . to you."

There was no time for the priest to read the final words of Danny O'Reilly and offer comfort to the widow. Mass said and the penitents dismissed, there were many who lingered long hours to speak privately with Father Patrick. It was a simple matter of the needs of the living having to come first. So it was near midnight before the priest reread the confession and went to find Jamie.

Jamie's lantern burned behind the blanket partition. She was awake; still dressed. He rapped softly on the tent pole.

He called to her in Gaelic, "You're awake, are you, my child?"

"Aye," she answered in a rusty voice.

"I need a word with you then. We shall speak in the Irish, for what I have to say is dangerous for both of us. Your husband knew this and so wrote his tale in the tongue of the homeland."

Carrying the lamp, she emerged from her space. The good father took the light from her and placed it on a wooden crate, then gestured for her to be seated on another upturned box.

"I have thought on the matter," Father Patrick continued. "There is much I cannot tell you, for the document contains the deepest secrets of a human heart. As such, it can be shared with God alone."

"Aye," she agreed quietly.

"This much I will say to you, girl. Your husband had a luxury few men are allowed. He knew his life was soon to be stolen from him and he had the time for reflection and true repentance. He died in grace, forgiven."

Jamie crossed herself and wept softly in relief. That was some consolation at least. "Tell me all you can, Father."

"The reason none have known where to find him is because he lived and died under a different name, in a manner of speaking. He reversed his Christian name from Daniel Robert to Robert Daniels, and stopped it there. This, he explains in his letter, was to keep shame from the house of O'Reilly."

"Shame?" she repeated hoarsely. "But what shame could there be in the soul of one so good and true?"

At this the priest stood silent. "In the hearts of all men there is some darkness; some yielding to temptation. For some it is pride or lust or greed. Sin is sin, all equal, in the eyes of our Lord. Each act of wrongdoing is one more blow of the hammer that drove the spikes into the hands of our Savior. Jesus died to take the eternal punishment for Daniel's sin before Daniel was called to account for it. It is enough that you know your husband recognized his guilt at the end, confessed it to our Lord, and repented. Daniel turned his back on the evil which enslaved him. He paid for his desertion with his very life. In so doing, he found eternal life. His reward is likely to be different from that of the men who murdered him."

"Murdered." The word fell heavily upon her.

"Aye. I can tell you no more, but when we leave here we will journey to Marysville. After that I must go straight to the government authorities and present information about grievous crimes."

Jamie had difficulty getting her thoughts around the truth. She sat in silent contemplation for a long time. The priest left her to her thoughts and waited patiently for the questions that must surely come.

So, Danny had been involved in something so terrible she could not know the truth of it. He had sold his soul and purchased it back at the price of his life. In the end he had once again come back to what he knew was right. *Robert Daniels he was called? Did any mourn him?* Jamie wondered.

After a while the priest returned. "I inquired about Robert Daniels. He was well known. Come the dawning Mayor North will take us to his grave and we shall mourn him properly together."

Mindful that he was in the presence of a recent widow, the mayor snapped off his top hat. Offering his arm to Jamie, they entered a weed-choked cemetery with Father Patrick following.

The mayor babbled cheerfully in the soft light of early morning, "Robert Daniels, ma'am. Everyone knew him. Everyone looked forward to his coming since he was the head teamster of Marrasco Freight Lines. 'Twas Robert who brought everything from whiskey to beans to shovels. Don't worry yourself that he went by another name. Men often change their names when they leave the States behind. I myself have done so because of an unfortunate incident back east. No fault of my own, of course, but it's sometimes healthier for a man to take up a new moniker when starting fresh."

"It did not prove to be healthy for my husband to do so," Jamie replied quietly.

"No. No, Missus O'Reilly. You are correct. That was not the case." He led her around a fresh mound of earth topped by a tilting cross. "Daniels . . . er . . . Mister O'Reilly came up against a bad run of luck and that's the plain truth of it. There he was one day, top man with Marrasco. Then he stops to water his mules with Gabby—"

The priest asked, "Gabby?"

"Gabby, we call him. Near as we can figure, he's Italian. Had his tongue cut out by Mescaleros back in '40. He can't read or write a stroke of English, and he don't speak, which makes him a good companion. Your husband liked him well enough. Bunked at Gabby's cabin when on the run up the mountain. Gabby is the one who found Daniels killed." Mayor North stopped as he gestured toward the grave where a weathered wooden marker displayed the inscription:

ROBERT DANIELS
Native of Ireland

In spite of the fact that Jamie had prepared herself for the sight, the reality of Danny's grave was like a blow to the stomach. Father Patrick moved quickly to her side and supported her.

The mayor said in a matter-of-fact way, "This is where we buried him. Of course there being no man of the cloth at hand for the services, we had to wing it, but we did the best we could. At that he got better than many; there's men who just up and disappear, between days, like we say. Who knows what becomes of them?"

Jamie questioned him. "You did not say . . . *how* he died."

"Carved up like a Christmas goose, ma'am. Somebody sure did not like him, although I cannot say who it was or why. A right personable fellow, Daniels was."

Jamie nodded and leaned her head against Father Patrick's shoulder. She had heard enough.

The priest thanked the mayor. "And now, sir, Missus O'Reilly needs time alone. If you would be so kind as to leave us."

The top hat was replaced and set straight with a tap of the mayor's hand. He bowed. "I've got business to tend to." Then to Jamie, "I can get you a special price on a marble headstone, if you're interested. Let me know and I'll see to it. The undertaker is a friend of mine. You might could get something off the shipping since your late husband worked steady for Marrasco."

With that Mayor North retreated down the hill and headed back toward town at a brisk pace. Jamie sighed and sat down on a flat rock a few paces from the grave.

"I cannot believe that it is Danny there." She searched the face of the priest. "Can we be sure?"

"You may be certain of it, Jamie O'Reilly. Your search ends here."

"Murdered." She could scarcely say the word. "But who? You heard the mayor. Everyone liked him well enough."

Father Patrick pressed his lips together tightly. He did not reply, but Jamie sensed he knew much more than he could say.

Opening his prayer book, he replied, "Many are those who have come to these mountains in search of fortune. Many have perished at the hands of violent men and then been left to the wolves or been buried in unmarked graves. This service then, while read for Daniel Robert O'Reilly, must also be for those who are known only to God." He raised his eyes heavenward. "May God have mercy on their souls."

CHAPTER 9

As racc day neared, some amazing preparations went on to ready *New World* for the contest. I came on deck early on Sunday morning, even though it was supposed to be my day of rest, in order to watch the goings-on.

The first thing I noticed startled even me: The forward and aft cargo booms were being unshipped and lowered to the deck. These derricks were the method by which heavy freight was loaded into the hold. As I watched, the forward crane was hoisted aloft by means of an A-frame on the dock and set aside. Then the process was repeated with the one astern.

"What's going on?" I asked Gutterson, who was assisting with the dismantling.

Nuck rubbed his forelock briskly but did not stop heaving on the line. "Captain Wakeman's orders," he said. "To reduce the drag. Every piece of work that isn't needed comes down."

My intended question about the gingerbread trim topping the pilothouse died unasked. With the boom down and the A-frame pushed aside, I could see that the scalloped ornamentation had already been removed. Like a wrestler stripping for a bout, *New World* was rapidly getting in fighting array.

If the loss of the cargo booms was surprising, the amputation that followed was even more so. The crew dismembered the guards over the great paddle wheels. "Wakeman's orders," was all the explanation I got. The *World* no longer looked merely naked; she looked crippled or deformed somehow.

Wakeman himself showed up to supervise the process and I asked why I had not been informed. "Shouldn't the captain be notified before his ship is torn apart?" I queried, angry at being so ignored.

"The captain, yes," Wakeman agreed. "Not the pilot. Do well with this race and we'll see. Prove to me that you have enough backbone to be captain and then we'll see."

I had been demoted, just like that. "If you are going to captain, then perhaps I should stay behind," I said bluntly. "There is never room for two captains on the bridge at the same time."

Thankfully Wakeman looked dismayed. "Let's have no talk like that," he scolded. "You know the ship and you know the river. Where could I find someone now who knows both?"

"What about the booms?" I prodded, to see how far my momentary advantage went. "If she grounds on a bar, what tackle am I supposed to use to free her?"

"You just see that she doesn't ground!" Wakeman sputtered. "Listen: I was mate on the *Sultana* in '44 when she set the record from New Orleans to Natchez. Nineteen hours and forty-five minutes. And for that contest we shortened her stacks and scraped the gilt paint off her trappings!" Then turning away to show that our conversation was at an end, he ordered the lifeboats lowered from their davits and even their riggings removed.

I took myself belowdecks to keep from getting into a shouting match with Wakeman. I suppose I should have been grateful at all he was doing to help *New World* win the contest, but I cannot say I enjoyed his treatment of me.

Finding the engineer in his cubbyhole I asked if he knew of what was happening above. "Never mind, sonny," he said. "Let Mister Wakeman have his way. Not that it will make a pennyworth of difference. *World* is in fine fettle for racing." He patted the projecting steel hook of an eccentric arm with affection. "She could beat *Goliath* if she was carrying fifty tons of extra weight. Only two things make a difference, sonny."

"And what are those?" I asked, smiling.

"Trim," Olson said briefly, wiping his glistening pate with a palm as thick and greasy as a slab of bacon. "*World* spins along the best when she draws five feet and a half of water forward and five aft. We'll load her with a nicety to those levels."

"And the second thing?"

Olson paused to squint over his round spectacles. He never seemed to look through them, only pushing them up on his broad forehead or down on his stubby nose as occasion demanded. The present pose looked schoolmasterish. "The second thing is piloting," he allowed with a grimace, as if embarrassed that his finely tuned machinery should be in any way jeopardized by human miscalculation. "A good pilot will never let the rudder stay 'cross the stern a second longer than needed, sonny," he lectured. "Rudder drags anytime it's not amidships. Races get lost or won on judgment."

The chief engineer studied me as if I were a fragment of questionable equipment in need of regulating. I made up my mind to go ashore, where no one would think to judge my piloting ability until race time. But I could not resist asking, "And me? Does my judgment measure up?"

"Find out soon, eh sonny!" he said.

<hr/>

Race day morning dawned cloudless and still. The waters of the bay were flat calm, as if agreeing to do their part in seeing that the times were the fastest possible. The motionless atmosphere hung heavily on me as I rose in my cabin in the texas. Uncovering Scrimshaw's cage, I wondered if the quiet was a portent good or bad. Even the parrot seemed unusually subdued. He normally greeted the day with "hellos" past counting, but not this day. Everything was in a state of watchful waiting.

Soon a column of black smoke rose straight upward from the *World*'s stack. Olson must have tossed pitch pine into the furnace, so black and heavy was the plume. A few docks away, *Goliath*'s stoked boilers pierced the sky with a similar angry raven-colored spear. The competing javelins of smudge flattened against some invisible barrier in the air. The fumes joined and mingled, spreading out to become a dusky ceiling resting on twin pillars.

The docks grew crowded. Passengers jostled their way through spectators and pickpockets. Gamblers offered odds on any and all aspects of the race, from which boat would win, to the likelihood of a boiler exploding en route. Hawkers proclaimed the virtues of everything from dollar watches to patented coal-tar tonics guaranteed to give you the lung capacity of a steamboat.

Moving Scrimshaw to his perch in the pilothouse, I walked about the upper deck, studying the chaos below. I saw Olson directing with an iron hand the stowing of cargo, gear, and people. With a precise squint, he called for kegs of nails to be rolled aft, judged the effect on the waterline, then ordered them moved forward about six inches before nodding his satisfaction.

Elijah, dressed for the occasion in his finest white uniform, sounded a three-toned gong and proclaimed in a sonorous tone much like a foghorn, "If you ain't goin' with us, please to get ashore!" Grumbling sightseers slowly complied.

The movement of masses of humans rearranged Olson's loading. From the way the top of his head turned bright pink, I gathered that his poise was being strained. I saw him collar a pair of young men attempting to change from port to starboard. He gestured from them to the capstan where Gutterson stood holding a coil of line.

Even without being able to hear, I knew that he threatened them with being bound if they did not remain fixed in place.

At last all was in readiness, or at least as ready as could be managed. I was summoned to a meeting of the captains to take place under a red-and-white-striped awning.

Marrasco and I scowled at each other while a man named Bigler, a local politician and would-be candidate for governor, gave a speech. He droned on at length about how muscular competition was symbolic of the vitality of California and how California would soon be a state, leading the nation to new prosperity.

Two things occurred to mar the proceedings. About midway through Bigler's oration, prosperous and vital California had one of her periodic earthquakes. Nothing of great force or significance, but it made each man in the throng study his neighbor to see who was doing the shoving. More than one fight broke out as accusations were exchanged.

Bigler, being caught up in the throes of his own eloquence, had not felt the tremor. When he noted the quizzical looks on many faces and the lack of attention being paid his soaring climax, he stopped dead in the water, pondering whether perhaps he had misused the word *copious* or something.

Shortly thereafter, one of the rickety piers dating from Bear Flag Rebellion days collapsed under the weight of the audience. The dock, which had looked like a gap-toothed smile, was no great loss, but two hundred

onlookers floundering in the bay caused Bigler's speech-
ifying to end on a more humorous than dramatic note.

For me the only things of importance were the rules.
The race was to occupy two days, up and back. Time
would be kept of the arrival in Sacramento. The speedier
boat would then leave earlier on the downstream leg by
that much of an interval. The first to pass the finish at
Yerba Buena Island would be declared the winner.

The two boats backed into the bay, swung 'round in
the stream, and lined up on the official starter's craft.
Grandly proclaimed a "pinnace" on the broadsheets
tacked up by agents of both companies, the small craft
rocking in the swells was a three-thwart rowboat, overloaded with dignitaries in silk ties.

Besides the plumes of dark smoke, both *New World*
and *Goliath* sent shrieking jets of steam rushing from
their safety relief valves. In the starter's dinghy was a top-
hatted figure with a white flag at the end of a long pole.
I stood on the quarterdeck with one hand on the rope of
the signaling bell and the other on the wheel. What had
been continuous buzz and chatter from belowdecks quieted as the starter raised his banner, signaling us to get
ready.

Then with a rush the flag swooped down. Before it
had even described half its arc, I rang for full speed
ahead. Olson, anticipating the call, sent *New World*

surging forward before the last stroke had finished ringing.

At the same instant as the signal flashed, a cannon erupted on Telegraph Hill, letting the whole town know that the race was on. I saw the puff of gray smoke out of the corner of my eye. In two heartbeats the boom of the gun rolled out to me on the water, speeding us on our way.

Steamboats were deceptive creatures. The craft of the '50s looked ungainly and because of their size, appeared slow. With only sixty pounds of pressure exerted on their massive, single-cylinder pistons, the paddle wheels revolved at just sixteen turns a minute. But the amount of water they pushed was amazing.

The surge forward provided by the turn of the wheels pushed a mass of white water ahead of the steamer's broad forehead, like the whale lunging to swallow Jonah.

The air so still and cloudless, the bay unmasked by fog, the day had no need of chart or compass. Mount Diablo rose due east like a spike on which the morning hung. We shaped our course for San Pablo Point and the passage to the river proper.

By the time we had rounded the point and entered the Carquinez Strait, the *World* was two boat lengths ahead. We passed Benecia with whistles screaming, but made no move toward the port. For the race there would be no way-freight and no way-passengers. Despite our lack of neighborly regard, the arsenal at the fort saluted us with cannon fire.

Stripped of her wheel guards, *New World* threw

spray clear over the top of the upper deck. If there had been a boat afire anywhere near our course, the *World* could have extinguished the blaze without even slowing.

I can state without blushing that Marrasco was a deft hand at a tiller. His knowledge of the river was superior to my own, and he took advantage of every lee that presented itself to make up time. *Goliath* showed a turn of speed that I had not imagined she possessed, and Marrasco exploited unseen eddies to minimize the force of the current. The race bid fair to be quite a contest, and had me scratching my head about the outcome, particularly when the stream narrowed as we traveled farther upriver.

Fortunately, we were not without a few tricks of our own.

New World carried ample wood aboard to make the run to Sacramento without refueling. Such was not the strategy worked out by Olson and myself, however. Olson was emphatic that to keep in proper racing trim, we needed to wood up near the halfway mark. Without breathing a word of our intentions to another soul, I had contracted for a supply of fuel behind Decker Island.

We were booming along upriver at that point, still two lengths ahead of *Goliath*. When I put the helm hard over and scooted behind the point of the half-moon-shaped isle, Marrasco gave a savage shrill of the whistle. I had to smile. I was certain that signal was his victory cry, thinking I had made a wrong move at last. The current behind the island was slower, tempting to a novice pilot, but the channel was a good mile longer than the river itself; more than enough for *Goliath* to completely overtake *New World*.

In point of fact, if it had been necessary to moor up next to a woodpile, the *World* would have been at a real disadvantage when we reemerged onto the river. But the arrangements made with the woodyard man and his Miwok Indian laborers were different. They called for stove-length oak, seasoned and split, to be awaiting our arrival on a flat-bottomed barge!

We slowed just enough for Nuck Gutterson to make fast a line from the flatboat, and then it was full speed ahead once more. With the added drag of the barge, we were slowed considerably, but not for long. The squat, compact brown bodies of the Miwok Indians formed a bucket brigade. They pitched chunks of wood over the rail and passed it hand to hand to the aft companionway, to where Olson directed the stowage.

What with my attention divided between the waterway ahead and what was happening astern, I could not watch all the unloading. When next I looked aft, half the cords had disappeared into the hold, so rapidly and mechanically did the Miwoks work.

In under five minutes by the brass pilothouse chronometer, the wood was shifted, the barge cut loose astern, *New World* trimmed again to five and half-five, and the flatboat was being poled back ashore. Gutterson reported to me what my eyes had already noted and we surged forward with renewed speed.

When the hatch opened again on Nuck's heels, I thought he had forgotten something, but it was Elijah.

He was holding an enormous catfish by the gills, mindful of its spines. From its lively wiggles, it was clear the five-pound fish was very much alive. "Shore was a slick wooding up," he said with approval. "This here is for your supper after we catches and passes *Goliath*."

"Catfish aren't caught by trolling a line," I said. "Where'd you get that? Off the Miwoks?"

Elijah shook his head, a wide grin splitting his broad features. "*World* looks powerful ugly without her wheel guards," he observed, "but useful someways."

"How's that?"

"When we passed shoal water at the bottom of the island, that portside wheel shucked up a mess of catfish and throwed 'em up on the deck slicker'n Christmas." The starched whites of Elijah's uniform glowed with pride. He pointed ahead to *Goliath*'s impudent stern now two lengths ahead as we rejoined the main channel. "Mind you does your business, or you'll get beans!"

As if I had needed any further incentive to regain the lead.

Goliath was in the lead when we emerged from behind Decker Island and rejoined the battle. Our rendezvous with the wood flats left us a half mile to regain, but in high spirits. With *New World* back in trim, we were really booming along up the river. If Marrasco chanced to look over his shoulder, he would have seen us like an avenging fury, sweeping toward *Goliath* in a cloud of smoke, steam, spray, and flying catfish.

At each crossing of the current, we gained a little ground. Marrasco's piloting kept him to still water as much as possible, but every encounter with stiffer flow showed *New World*'s power.

When we reached Grand Island and the entry to Steamboat Slough, we were less than a quarter mile behind, with forty miles to go. That was when I knew with a certainty that Marrasco had indeed looked over his shoulder.

Something thudded against the wheelhouse just outside where I stood. The noise was of an invisible giant swinging a twelve-pound sledge into the timbers by my feet. Moments later, a second heavy slug, for such was the cause of the noise, smashed the glass of the pilothouse window, shattered a spoke of the wheel two rungs away from my left hand, and smacked into the back wall of the cabin.

Scrimshaw squawked and screeched. He had not been hit, but neither of us could count on continuing to have such luck. I scooped him off his brass perch and thrust him into Gutterson's arms. "Lock him in his cage," I shouted, "and send me Olson!"

A matter of a half minute was consumed in ducking out of the way, but it was enough to set the *World* crosswise of the river. Taking the full force of the current on her starboard bow, the steamer crabbed sideways, giving back a hundred yards of our gain.

Knowing that Marrasco, or his henchman, could not

possibly aim at that distance, it really did not matter if I stood left or right of the wheel. If I ducked down, I could not see to steer, so I ended up right back where I started, squarely in front of the window.

I was relieved when Olson showed up. He took one look at the splintered glass, then pivoted to take in the fist-sized cavity gouged from the oak plank wall. From the way he sputtered, stuttered, and snorted, I thought he was taking a conniption fit. Then he squared away his rage and came ahead on course. "So we got him scared, eh, sonny? What's your plan?"

"Can you keep the balance if the passengers are topside?" I asked.

He smiled, having tumbled at once to my scheme. "I'll send 'em right now," he allowed.

"Only volunteers," I cautioned. "This is a shooting war, you know."

"Sonny," he said, spitting tobacco juice ringing into the gaboon. "Sonny, any what won't volunteer will find it's a long swim to Sacramento."

Before long the narrow catwalk that fronted the pilothouse was packed with sightseers. Some of them looked askance at the busted glass, but only one protested the new arrangement. A pair of grizzled miners with their beards tucked inside their shirtfronts grabbed the reluctant soldier and held him upright between them. "Never you mind," one of them remarked loudly to the fearful young man. "It'd be bad press to kill payin' customers." Such was exactly my thinking as well.

"But what if somebody aims for the pilot and hits me instead?" This was also an echo of my own thoughts.

"Well, then," the second bewhiskered prospector replied. "We'll see you get a real wingding of a funeral, and this here steamboat'll wear black bunting all over the rails in yore honor."

I am sure he took great comfort from that. Fortunately for the worried gold seeker, my plan worked. No more shots were fired from *Goliath*. I did my piloting peering around the shoulders and hairy faces of my impromptu guards.

By the time we reached the point where Steamboat Slough rejoined the river proper, *New World* was breathing down *Goliath*'s neck. Marrasco had given up cautious steering and was attempting to prevent our passage by zigging back and forth. Knowing that he would endeavor to crowd us over when we made our move, I was content to hang back and let him wear himself out trying to anticipate our course.

Nuck Gutterson was back in the wheelhouse, ready to carry out such orders as needed dispatched. As the miles rolled by and we languished behind, he fretted that I had lost my nerve. Several times I noted him begin to speak, then draw back from challenging me.

When we drew abreast of the entrance to Babel Slough and only eight miles of race remained, he could hold his peace no longer. Tugging at his forelock till I thought he would scalp himself, he bobbed and wagged respectfully and said, "Begging your pardon, Mister Rafer, sir. But ain't we gonna run out of river?"

"That we are, Nuck," I agreed. "But don't worry, I know what I'm about."

On early trips I had studied a shoal place just below the high ridge called Sutterville. There had been plenty of water there on previous journeys, but the lead showed only four feet on the last passage. I also knew that the river had dropped still farther.

Timing was everything now. As the *World* approached the dead cottonwood that I had earlier marked by eye for this occasion, I roused from my seeming lethargy. Ringing the bell for more speed, I even dispatched Nuck to carry the word personally to Olson. "Tell him to give it all she's got, and watch for my next signal," I ordered. "Go!"

Her bow angled toward *Goliath*'s port side, *New World* belched a denser cloud of smoke and leaped forward. Marrasco, lulled somewhat by how we had hung back, was slow to react. When he did catch sight of our run, I could picture him spinning his wheel hard aport to jam us toward the bank.

The miners on deck jeered and yelled at *Goliath*'s move, but they also linked their arms around guywires and turned posts. "Best hold on," one warned. "We're gonna crack like two eggs and see which is got the tougher shell!"

It was my fervent prayer that a collision was not about to happen, but the next few seconds would tell.

Keeping the *World* on course meant that the other steamer was sliding closer and closer. The churning wheel menaced our flank like a meat grinder. I expected that Marrasco would try to panic me by turning even sharper across our bow; I not only expected it, I was counting on it.

When it happened I rang the signal bell like fury to set the World hard back. At the same instant I cramped the wheel to starboard. To the passengers it must have seemed that I had taken leave of my senses, deliberately turning into the path of disaster.

Ponderous and dangerously deliberate was the World's response. Then as the forward way came off her and Olson set her full astern, I flung the wheel the other way. The bow swung even sharper to starboard, clearing Goliath's port side by inches.

That was only half the plan. Unimpeded by the other ship's stern, I rang up full speed ahead again. Broadside to the current and leaping out toward the middle of the river, New World lost ground, spinning downstream as if running away.

The miners on board with me gave up a collective groan, certain that they had backed a loser. That was the instant that Goliath ramped upward on her port side as she ran full tilt onto the sandbar.

Canted at a funny angle, Marrasco tried to remedy his dilemma by coming ahead and running off the bar. What he had failed to notice was precisely what I had explored on earlier trips: The sandbank followed the eastward curve of the river and when Goliath attempted to turn back into the channel, she ran squarely across the bar.

Minutes later the World had recovered from her

sideslip and was again on course, headed upriver. There was loud shouting and cheering from our customers, matched by stoney silence from the throng on the other ship. That was the moment when I was most glad for all the company on the hurricane deck. I have no doubt that otherwise the wheelhouse and I would have been ventilated for keeps.

Marrasco was a savvy enough pilot to maneuver *Goliath* off the shoal in only a short while. He gave chase again at once, but the damage was done. *New World* showed only her heels from that point on until we steamed into Sacramento City, ten minutes in the lead on the first leg of the race.

CHAPTER 10

That night I posted a guard around *New World*. It was at Wakeman's insistence; I did not really believe that Marrasco would try to sabotage the boat or set fire to it, but . . .

Olson vowed to stay on board and sleep in the engine room. Nuck Gutterson and three other deckhands divided the night into four watches and they patrolled in pairs.

I remained in my cabin with Scrimshaw, entertaining dinner guests. No females, though the thought did cross my mind. I really wished Mrs. O'Reilly had an identical twin, or a sister at the very least, but there was no luck to be had.

Apart from Nuck Gutterson and Elijah, I had no one close enough to call friends on the whole Pacific coast. Enemies were in more plentiful supply.

It was with the idea of widening my circle of acquaintances who would not put bullets through pilothouse windows that two men joined me for supper. My dinner party consisted of editor Alfred Squires of the *Independent* and old man Leidesdorf, former steamer master and merchant.

"Ah," sighed Squires, pushing back his plate. "My compliments to the chef. As fine a repast as any west of New Orleans."

Leidesdorf, fingers greasy from plucking fried catfish and hush puppies from the heaping bowls, nodded his agreement, but continued eating. The man positively expanded as he got around such good eating. The color in his face heightened until the tracery of veins on his nose disappeared.

"Tell me, Captain Maddox," Squires said. "What will be the outcome of tomorrow's race?"

Puzzled at the question, I retorted, "We're going to win, of course. Given our lead time, and a downstream channel, *New World* will never even look back."

"You mistake me," Squires corrected. "What I mean to ask about is the aftermath of your victory. What do you think will be the result?"

Scrimshaw had been anxiously pacing from one foot to the other. Sliding my chair away from the table, I gave the blue and gold bird a choice of snacks while I thought about my reply. Scrimshaw first beaked a morsel of corn dodger, tossed it aside and eagerly grabbed a hunk of succulent fish in his left claw. "I intend to settle the issue of the fastest boat once and for all," I said. "Then this racing nonsense will stop before someone gets hurt."

Leaning back, Squires drew a thin cigar from his brocade vest. He looked at me for permission to light it, which I gave. Flicking a match against his thumbnail, he first blew a smoke ring and then said, "Captain, you may know a great deal about steamers and rivers, but you still have much to learn about men. Don't you think Marrasco will seek revenge? After having been the cock of the walk around here, do you suppose he'll just give up? Not on your tintype."

Leidesdorf wiped his hands on his pantlegs and looked longingly at the unlit cigar that remained in Squires's pocket. "It's true, vhut he says," Leidesdorf agreed. "Marrasco is like the fighting cock, or maybe the badger. Quit is not in him, unt there is no end to his meanness."

Leidesdorf's support of Squires met with the editor's approval. The newspaperman extended a cigar and a match. "And another thing," Squires took up the tale again. "Where is it printed that no new challenger can step up and toe the mark? Why, there'll be captains lining up to take you on the day after you get back to Frisco."

This was a hull-busting reef in the pleasant stream of my thinking. I had wanted nothing more than to end foolish conflict and keep the river safe for all. Instead, it seemed my course was having the opposite effect. My own pride had gotten me into a fix. Winning the race would widen the war. Losing would cost me my job.

I must have looked glum, because Squires said, "It'll come right in the end. As soon as there's enough boats operating, cutthroat competition will have to end and sense come to the Sacramento River. But not yet. Not," he added significantly, peering up at me from under his

bushy eyebrows, "Not, I fear, without disaster for someone."

No matter how much I wanted to get a good night's
sleep before the race resumed, slumber absolutely eluded
me. I tossed fitfully in my bunk, thinking of all that
Squires had said, about the contest, about Wakeman and
Agent Gillis, and about Marrasco. When I tried to force
my schooner of a brown study into more pleasant channels, I got melancholy remembering my boyhood home.
Then Jamie O'Reilly came to mind, which was no help at
all. I got up.

My feet slapping on the plank deck startled
Scrimshaw into inquiring "Hello?" He subsided again at
once under the cloth that covered his cage. At least one
of us was able to sleep.

Nuck Gutterson was making his rounds of the main
salon, where I joined him. "Everything quiet, Nuck?" I
asked.

"All quiet," he agreed. "After your friends left, only
had one more visitor. But he's gone now."

"Oh? Who was that?" The way Nuck screwed up his
face reminded me that he had trouble recollecting names.
"Never mind," I hurriedly amended my question. "What
did he want?"

"Engineer off *Goliath*," he said. "I disremember his
name. Come to see Olson."

Jumping to my feet I grabbed Nuck and shook him. "You let him on the boat? Where'd he go?"

"Whillikers, Rafer, Captain, sir," Nuck stuttered, alternately pulling his forelock and bobbing his head. "Me and Quinn searched him. He din't have nothing on him but a bottle. Said he come to hoist a few with Olson; show there was good sports on both sides . . . not like Marrasco, he said."

"Olson agreed to this?" I asked suspiciously.

Nodding vigorously, Nuck continued. "Olson come up on deck and escorted the feller down personally."

"Go get Quinn," I ordered, directing Nuck to call the other deckhand on watch. Quinn, when I quizzed him, confirmed everything Nuck had reported, and added one more bit of news. "Mister Olson whispered to me," Quinn explained. "Said he could pick this other engineer's brains. Find out their strategy like. Said not to worry about a thing."

Of Olson's loyalty and good intentions I had no doubts, but letting a competitor on board gave me concerns for our engineer's safety. "Run down to his berth and check on Olson," I directed Nuck, sending Quinn back topside.

"Sleeping like a baby," Gutterson reported a few minutes later. "Now you go do the same, Rafer, Captain, sir."

The downstream leg of the race was due to get under way at precisely ten in the morning. That is to say, *New*

World would stir up the water en route for San Francisco at four bells; *Goliath* would attempt to catch us after starting ten minutes past the hour.

Barring something unforeseen, like shucking a paddle wheel or running over a sailing barge, there was no way we could lose. But when I ordered engineering to get up a head of steam and hold it at fifty-six pounds, no aye-aye was returned on the signal bell.

It was one hour until race time and I could not understand the lack of a response. Could it be that the bell cable was fouled and Olson could not make out my alert? It seemed to me that the engineer was as anxious to win this contest as I was and would also be paying close attention to the time.

Entering the gangway leading down to the engine room, I ran headlong into Nuck Gutterson. "Cap'n," he blurted urgently. "We got trouble."

"What sort of trouble?" An anxious knot formed instantly in the pit of my stomach, just as if I had swallowed a cannonball.

"The black gang never came back last night, nor this morning neither. Shall I go hunt for them?"

Weighing the chances of Nuck finding the stokers versus the likelihood that he would not return either, I belayed his suggestion. "They are drunk or prisoner," I said. "Either way you wouldn't find them till after the race was lost. Where's Olson?"

"Sleepin'," was the fearful reply.

I exploded. "Did you try to rouse him?"

"Yessir," Nuck reported. "He just won't be roused."

There had been something pernicious in last night's friendly drink with the competition after all. While not dead, Olson might as well have been a corpse for all the good he was. His sonorous breathing and the trail of drool down his cheeks convinced me: Trying to change that hunk of flesh into an alert engineer was futile.

"Nuck," I said, working to stay calm and sound composed. "Drag Mister Olson to the crew quarters so he's out of the way. Bring all the deckhands except two back down here with you. I'll start feeding the fire, then you take over quick as you can."

"But Captain, I ain't no engineer, and neither is Quinn."

"Don't fret," I told him. "You just stoke like I tell you and leave the rest to me."

Marrasco's scheming knew no limits. If bullets and collisions would not serve his turn, then poisoning my engineer and kidnapping my crew would work as well. But I intended to show him differently. Luckily we still had plenty of time to get up a head of steam. Once under way, I had no doubt that the hands could keep the fire going. Given our ten-minute lead, we would win despite Marrasco's conniving.

At five minutes before the hour, I shouted, "Cast off forward . . . cast off stern. Pole her away from the dock!" Then I ran back down to the engine room, shouldering passengers aside.

Grabbing Nuck by the shoulders I looked him square in the face. "Take the wheel," I ordered. "Pilot her dead center down channel."

"But Rafer . . ."

"Do it!" I screamed, then softer, "Just keep her to midstream for a minute or two. There are no bars or crossings on this stretch of water and I'll be back up before you know it."

The cause of all this running around was mechanical. Getting a steamboat into motion was not a simple proposition like clucking to a four-up team or setting a sail.

Firing the boiler turned water into steam right enough, but moving from there to the spinning of the paddle wheels was the trick. I spat on my hands and grabbed the steel rod called a Johnson bar from its rack on the wall.

Glancing at the gauge, I noted that the pressure was up. The clock showed thirty seconds before ten.

Placing the Johnson bar against the valve shaft on the floor, I heaved upward with all my strength. This motion opened an intake valve to the giant cylinder, letting live steam flood in. Of course I was also lifting half the weight of the walking beam, suspended in its gallows frame on the hurricane deck thirty feet over my head.

When the cylinder stroke had reached its maximum, I levered the Johnson bar down. This reverse motion opened the exhaust valve for the fully expanded steam and forced live steam into the opposite end of the cylinder. It was my weight along with my back and shoulder muscles against the inertia of the machinery.

Each cycle of up bar and then down bar, turned the crank a little faster as the steam power took over an increasing share of the work. At the dozenth stroke, the walking beam was well into its swing.

That was the point at which I yelled to Quinn, "Hook 'em up!" and he slammed home the fasteners of the connecting rods. From that moment on, the spin of the rocker eccentrics would open and close the valves by means of projections called wipers. The paddle wheels were turning and the race was on.

For all the grandeur of being called captain, it was a less than glorious launch. I left instructions for Quinn to keep an eye on the steam gauge and the water clock, never letting the one below fifty pounds of pressure nor the other below half full of water for the boiler.

Sacramento had no signal gun to give us an official starting signal, so some wag lit off a string of Chinese firecrackers by ten of the watch. Of course, the fact that he fired the string in the middle of a crowd caused almost as much excitement as the dock's collapse back in Frisco, but I did not see it. I heard about it from a very relieved Nuck Gutterson.

It was my intention to hold to a steady but not extravagant pace. The last thing I wanted to risk was an equipment failure that would turn certain victory into inglorious defeat. If we needed a turn of speed, I knew that the *World* had plenty in reserve.

There is a sharply curved oxbow bend in the river about a mile north of the entrance to Elk Slough. The

Sacramento turns abruptly northwest, pivots south around a point of land heavily screened with willows, and then just as suddenly, turns back northeast. The half loop takes a thousand yards of river, but leaves the sailor a scant five hundred feet across the narrow neck from where he entered the crook of waterway.

With Olson snoring loudly in a hammock aft, Quinn and others force-feeding the boiler fires, me piloting, and Nuck running up and down gangways to keep me informed, we were still winning the race. Our passengers did not seem to recognize anything unusual in our behavior. They were busy laughing and swapping stories about debts of food and drink to be collected from *Goliath*'s backers.

New World had ample fuel to make the run back to the bay. Had Olson been conscious, we would have repeated our trick with the wood barges, but as things stood, I trusted to our lead and the help of the current to keep us ahead.

The river at the oxbow bend is plenty wide enough for traffic to pass with room to spare, but it is not ample for three boats abreast. When *New World* reached the apex of the curve, I found the river ahead blocked.

A freight schooner was being passed on its outboard rail by the slim steamer *Antelope*. While there was plenty of time to slow and avoid a collision, there was only a split second to decide between steering and seeing to the engines. I could not do both.

I made my choice.

Seeing that I might have to trim the branches of the

willows, I said to Gutterson, "Go below. Tell Quinn to close the throttle and open the steam relief valve." Nuck sprinted for the engine room.

Steering for the far shore, I let the current push the *World* across the path of the other ships, knowing that their captains would be turning into the force of the stream to slow them down. Disturbed, but not unduly alarmed, I waited for the high-pitched shriek of the steam relief valve.

It never came.

Many explosions on side-wheelers like *New World* happened when slowing. All the expansive power of steam capable of turning forty-foot-wide paddles could never be ignored safely; it had to go somewhere.

Ringing the signal bell only reminded me that there was no one below who knew what I was trying to communicate. I wasted precious seconds before abandoning the wheel to run aft shouting "Nuck! Quinn! The relief valve! Turn the handle of the relief . . ."

I had descended only one level, pushing through stunned travelers milling about the salon, when there came a deep rumble from inside the bowels of the ship. It was as if a volcano were brewing in the *World*'s belly.

Panicked passengers overwhelmed my progress toward the gangway, throwing me back as they sensed an imminent disaster. There was a roar from below, and then an anguished scream, cut off by a bellow of steam and a jet that shot from the starboard side of the hull.

New World drove her bow up across shoal water and into a gooseberry patch. The scrape tossed the customers around and buried me under a pile. *World*'s naked starboard wheel ground to a stop on the riverbank, and then the movement ceased.

Antelope, which had steered successfully between the pilotless rush of *New World* and the sailing vessel, witnessed the explosion and turned back to help. Because of a weak spot in the steam condenser chamber, only that tank had blown, rather than the boiler itself.

If the boiler had disintegrated, it would have carried away all three decks above it and killed or injured hundreds. As it was, only one was hurt: Nuck Gutterson. It was his scream of agony I had heard as he was scalded. He died in my arms.

My first thought, when I was able to think again at all, was that Nuck Gutterson had given his life for me. If I had left him at the wheel, it would have been me in the engine room.

My second thought was that he was somehow responsible for his own death. I had told him to open the relief valve; I knew I had. I remembered it.

Then Quinn gave me the word. Gutterson and he had tried to open the valve, but spinning the wheel made no difference. In Quinn's opinion, "Somebody jiggered the relief pipe. As long as it was open it stayed so, but shut it once and it could not be opened again."

Of course after the damage caused by the explosion, there were too many things wrecked in the engine room to know for certain. Quinn and two stokers had gotten out unscathed only by running.

Gutterson had remained behind, trying to the last to release the stuck valve.

I was discharged, of course. Wakeman said nothing about Nuck's death or the explosion, neither of which could be called my fault. I was fired for losing the race, and told to count myself lucky I was not arrested for leaving the wheel untended.

Lucky.

CHAPTER 11

More about my life changed because of that ruptured steam line than just the loss of my position. I had followed no trade but shipping, knew no profession except piloting. Two weeks of trying convinced me that no one connected with river traffic would hire me. Though no court convicted me and indeed, none existed in which I could be tried, Gillis spread the word that I and I alone had caused death, destruction, and shame.

Worse still was that I believed it myself. I had been *New World*'s captain. If I had demanded that no one come aboard and allowed no one to leave, then no sabotage would have been possible. Nuck Gutterson would still be alive.

I gave Scrimshaw to Elijah. "I'm going to the gold-fields," I vowed. "If I can pan out enough for passage to anywhere, I'm leaving the West forever. Going where nobody has ever heard of me. In any case, I can't take care of the bird. He's yours, 'Lijah."

The cook shook his head ponderously. "I's leavin' the

boat too," he vowed. "It ain't right what they doin' to you."

"You won't have any trouble catching on with another steamer."

"Mebbe," he said slowly. "An' mebbe I'll start an eatery ashore. I ain't decided yet."

I had to smile. "Either way, Scrimshaw will be happy. Just remember to slip him a sardine."

"'Deed I will. God bless you, Rafer."

"And you, Elijah."

So having buried one friend, I parted from the other two. I suppose I could have returned to Sacramento and sought advice from Leidesdorf and Squires, but I could not bring myself to do so. I did not know if they blamed me for the tragedy, but I was afraid to find out.

Taking the little pay I had coming, and selling off my traps, I outfitted myself as a prospector and headed upriver. Walking was my mode of transport. I was as green a hand as any in the hills, but it was all I could think to do.

On my third night on the trail, I fell into company with a party of two men, brothers, from Pennsylvania. They were on their way back east. They were not being wafted homeward in a servant-attended carriage, but neither were they dressed in rags. Though lean of frame and face, they looked healthy enough.

They were reluctant to reveal the details of their

fortunes with a stranger, but I managed to swap fresh flour for stories; flapjacks for fables, I suppose.

Ben, the elder, said, "We've had plenty of California. Gonna go back to farming, which is what we know. Made enough to pay off eighty acres, buy the dairy from Father, settle down. Lord, how I miss Sally, that's my wife. Four letters in fourteen months is all. Bess, that's our little girl, be two next Christmas Eve. She'll not even know me, though Sally says the baby kisses my picture every night and cries when she hears a knock at the door . . . thinking it's me come home."

The face of this sinewy man was covered in wire-brush whiskers. His phiz appeared to have spent fourteen months unacquainted with any razor. His hands—calloused, leathery, the tip of one little finger missing—were the fists of a man twice his age if I reckoned rightly. He stropped a butcher knife against the top of his mule-ear boots and . . . a tear rolled down his cheek as he spoke of his family.

Which was worse? I wondered. *To miss your own terribly, knowing that they prayed for your safe return, or to have no one who cared about you at all?*

The younger brother, Arnie, spoke up, hurriedly taking over their tale, as if to deflect embarrassment from his sibling. "Came close to a really big strike lots of times," Arnie said. "Next claim over from ours up on the American River, man took out a whole pound of gold from a space no bigger than this." With his hands he described a washtub-sized hole. "Early on we did well enough; even in the days when flour was five dollars a pound, we made out so as to eat and put a little away besides."

"I'm bound up the American," I volunteered. "I heard tell there's still claims to be had around Hangtown."

Both brothers shook their heads. "Times is harder now," Arnie continued. "Can't dig in gullies and dry canyons and wash out enough to get by. Only gold now is in the river. You gotta move rocks, build dams, divert the flow so as to get under things that ain't been dry since Methuselah was a pup. Anyway, that's why we called it quits. Too late for this year anyhow and next season is too long away. My gal, Corrie, she might not wait forever."

"Why too late?"

"Water coming down the canyons is already high. Rains could start most anytime," Ben explained. "Most everybody either heads out or holes up somewhere warm and dry till next April."

This brought the conversation to a halt, while Ben sliced the slab of bacon, tossing the pieces to Arnie to fry. I stirred a mess of fixings to cook up in the bacon grease. "Hangtown is a regular place now," Ben resumed. "Five thousand folks, give or take, fifty saloons, five hundred gamblers."

"If not there, then where?" I inquired.

Ben squinted at the fire, then turned toward his brother. "That feller we met up Coloma way . . . Swede, I think."

"Norwegian," Arnie corrected. "Tolliver, his name

was. Runs an express over the mountains. He hears most all the news. Anyway, he says the Yuba River is the place now. Up above Marysville. But I still think the water will run you out."

"Maybe not," Ben disagreed. "Not if you get lucky in a place ain't been turned over too many times."

"That's good enough for me then," I said.

"Rafer, would you object to some advice?" Ben asked apologetically. California was a great place for minding your own business; it was the safest course.

"I'm the tenderfoot here," I said. "Speak your mind plainly and I'll listen."

"There's three kinds of men in these hills: Them as gets a bellyful and quits, like us. Them as tries their hands at prospecting, then figures right away to make more selling to or stealing from the miners. And lastly there's them who thinks the next canyon over, the next riffle in the creek, the next hullabaloo, is gonna make their pile for them. Rafer, them third ones never gets home atall . . . cholera, Injuns, snakebite, scurvy . . . something always carries them off. Mind you ain't one."

Several more days of travel brought me to the town of Yuba City, near the confluence of the Yuba and Feather Rivers, not far from Marysville. There was a steamer chuffing slowly up to the dock there; this a good fifty miles farther upriver from Sacramento City. She was the *Linda*, named for someone's sweetheart, no doubt. I hoped that the comparison did the lady in question an injustice, since the boat was a pitiful wreck of a stern-wheeler only one cabin high above the main deck. She looked to be about one-sixth the size of *New World*. Then the thought struck me: It was no concern of mine, not anymore.

I had heard tell that the river was navigable up this far and even farther. There would be profit in it for opening up the northern mines. Reduced freight and lower passage rates would improve the lot of the miners in those parts, which now included me I remembered with chagrin.

An Irishman operated a ferry across the river near the makeshift wharf. For ten cents I climbed aboard a water-logged raft and the ferryman switched an old blind mule who stood on a treadmill. The animal's lumbering plodding gait turned a drum around that was looped to a cable. This was the motive of power by which I crossed the stream. I pointed my thumb toward the shacks of the town. "Growing much?" I asked, by way of conversation.

The Irishman spat noisily into the river. "Bless you, sir," he said, "that it tis, devil take the landlords. One year ago it was naught but an Injun village and a corral. Now look at it."

It was difficult to understand what it was about a few clapboard houses and mud streets that provoked so much hostility. "Why so angry? Seems to me the more citizens, the greater call for your services."

"Aye, but I had me a tent pitched yonder just by that

big oak there, where you see the blacksmith shop and the newspaper office."

"So?"

"Do you understand nothing, man?" he demanded. "I left the place to go off a-prospecting. When I come back they was selling lots here for twenty-five dollars apiece! Laid out a town right where my tent had been. Made twenty-five thousand dollars they say. And me? I earned nothing for my pains but a case of scurvy!"

I prudently kept mum thereafter about the growth of Yuba City.

When the boatman landed me, I could not help but study the stern-wheeler at closer range. Professional curiosity, I suppose. Then I faced east and thought once more about my mining destination. If I followed the Yuba River I would reach the town of Nevada in another forty miles or so. It had been my original goal and something about it still seemed to be calling me. I weighed this unknown attraction against the advice offered by the brothers Ben and Arnie.

There was a cry of "Look out!" and then a crash on the dock behind me. A rope sling had unraveled and a crate being unloaded from the *Linda* fell heavily on the wharf. When the box burst open it spilled a half dozen thin slabs of stone across the planks. There was the sound of violent cursing and a man dressed all in black shook his fist at the stevedore operating the block and tackle. "You dunderhead," he said (that was the mildest descriptive he employed), "you ignorant son of perdition. Don't you know that marble cost me a hundred and twenty dollars plus shipping all the way from Vermont? I can't sell them if they're busted!"

Another onlooker explained what the hooraw was about. "Headstones," he said, indicating the slabs of rock. "Kleinman there is the undertaker. He's probably lying about them costing him a double eagle apiece, but he can charge more now that he's announced it."

"Is there a lot of call for his services here?" I asked.

My informant, a smallish man with an upturned nose, shrugged. "One of them is mine," he said. He caught the glint of humor in my eye. "Not mine personally, you understand," he hastened to add. "My partner's. It was my promise to his dying self that I'd see him marked proper." From his shirtpocket he drew a scrawled note setting forth his partner's name and date of death. Beneath the date it proclaimed, *Gone but not forgotten.* "His own choice of sentiments too," he added.

I watched as the little man scurried over to the undertaker, indicated an undamaged stone and handed over the paper.

Kleinman nodded and the two shook hands. The surviving partner returned to my side. "Well, I'm headed back to my claim. I'll come back in two weeks when the carving is done and pay for it."

"What did your partner die of?"

"Say, are you a miner?" the little man inquired. "Have you got a claim hereabouts?"

"Just arrived," I said. "Thinking of prospecting the Yuba, up Marysville way."

"Just a minute," he said, laying his hand on my arm.

"You're a strapping, strong-looking fellow. Now that Jed is no more . . . ." There was a decent pause while he looked at the swirling waters. "I need some help working our . . . my claim up on the Feather. Stringtown it's called. What do you say? Care to throw in with me?"

And with that my destination was decided.

CHAPTER 12

My new partner, whose name I discovered was Alonzo Root, was a Missourian by birth, a cobbler by profession, and a talker by disposition. All these traits I discovered at once. As time went by I learned about one more facet of his personality: He was an extravagant expander of the truth. "Gold nuggets in the Feather River is big as peas and beans," he said. "Sometimes peach pits. Turn over any rock and you'll find some. You can't miss."

When I asked if he could show me samples, he agreed at once, then patted himself all over as if he could not remember where he kept his gold. Reaching at last into the smallest pocket of his waistcoat, he produced a square of paper folded seven times until it had reached postage stamp size. Alonzo looked up and down the road several times, then drew me aside into a clump of willows before unfolding the tiny parcel.

When the last layer had been unwrapped, after many dramatic pauses and renewed surveillance of the public thoroughfare, Alonzo at last revealed his secret. A pile of dull golden grains lay exposed to the light. The flakes were in size and quantity such as might spill from an accidental overturning of a salt shaker and be blown off a table without thought. "See," he said in a proud whisper, "see how coarse the grains? This came from one shovelful up to the claim."

"What about the pea-sized nuggets?" I inquired.

"Can't carry them around with me, no sir," he said, glancing over his shoulder. "Too heavy and too valuable. Got 'em hid near the claim."

Stringtown, when we arrived there, proved to be aptly named. I do not know if the moniker related to some early settler, but the "town" was a single line of shanties and huts that followed the curve of the river. A gravel bar some twenty yards wide paralleled the northern shore and it was this specimen of geology that drew the miners.

There were one-room cabins with clapboard walls and split cedar roofs. There were canvas-topped huts with cowhide walls. These constructions, together with a few tents and a handful of Indian bark huts constituted the metropolis of Stringtown.

The river in front of me was a tributary of the Feather. More specifically, it was the Middle Fork of the South Fork of the Feather River. This far up in the hills the prospectors had used up all their imagination. When it came to creeks there was no wordcraft left at all.

To introduce me to my new home, Alonzo took me to the local grocery and dry goods store: Jameson's Grand Emporium it was called. There was nothing grand about the establishment except its name. It too was housed in a structure that was more tent than building. The walls were made of green cowhide lashed with rawhide laces to an arch of peeled white alder trunks.

Out front of Jameson's store was a sign lettered in bad spelling and worse penmanship, TADAY— UNYUNS—FORE BITS. "That's crazy," I said. "Fifty cents for a single onion?"

"Ha!" Alonzo laughed. "That's nothing! Last winter, onions, when you could get 'em at all, was a dollar. Either way, it still means in gold dust. And boots going for forty dollars a pair . . . if I only had my tools!"

Jameson, the owner of the store, was a man of my height with brown hair and beard shading to gray. He had a friendly smile and an easy manner when Alonzo introduced me as his new partner. "New partner, eh?" Jameson said. "Welcome. You too, Alonzo. Glad you came back." It might have been my imagination, but Jameson's greeting of my coworker was a touch less enthusiastic than the one given me.

"We'll be needing some supplies," Alonzo continued, all unnoticing of any chill in the air. "Flour, beans, salt, coffee, salt pork . . . that ought to do it for now."

Jameson nodded and began heaping canvas sacks of grocery goods on a rough-hewn plank counter. Then he wet the stub of a pencil with his tongue and began writing in his account book.

"We'll pick it up in a few minutes; just want to take care of some business next door first," Alonzo said. "Oh, Rafer, sign that, will you? Then follow me."

Next door to the general store was a saloon and

gambling hall. As far as the construction and appearance of the two businesses, they were identical. But they differed in what was offered: The timber shelving in the tavern was lined with clay jugs with handles instead of pickle crocks. The slabs of redwood that served as tables were occupied by miners drinking and bucking the tiger in games of faro, rather than displays of picks and shovels.

Alonzo was hailed by several prospectors when he entered the shack, and was invited to come and have a drink. The bartender was bearded and longhaired, and therefore indistinguishable from all the others. Except for the bung starter thrust through the rope that served him as a belt and the fact that he stood between the customers and the clay jugs, there was no contrast.

"That'll be fifty cents," the saloon keeper growled, indicating a small pan balanced on the edge of the bar.

"No credit here like at the store?" I said to Alonzo.

"Black-hearted Yankee abolitionist, trusts nobody from the South," Alonzo whispered back. "I don't suppose you could . . ."

"You know I don't have any dust on me," I protested. "What about your sample?"

Alonzo shushed me hurriedly. "Never mind, then," he said in a hurt tone. Then louder he stated, "We'll come back later. Come on, Rafer. Let's gather our supplies and head to the cabin."

The cabin, as Alonzo so proudly named it, was a hole dug into the side of a dirt bank. Its entrance was covered with a pile of brush and pine boughs. It ran back into the hard-packed soil for about twenty feet. In the center of the floor was a firepit directly beneath a hole punched in the ceiling for a chimney. On either side of the fire were two blankets. Those rags and some cooking gear completed our domestic arrangements.

"Make yourself comfortable," Alonzo said, indicating one of the threadbare blankets. "Say, why don't you take the first turn at cooking, while I grab a little shut-eye? The old arrow wound I got in the Blackhawk War still pains me when I travel far. You don't mind, do you? It's too late to work the claim tonight. We'll go out first thing in the morning."

<hr>

The smell in the cave when I woke, compounded of wood smoke and other, less pleasant odors, drove me outside before the sun was up. I stretched in the crisp morning air and noticed that the riverbank was already ringing with the noises of mining tools.

Gathering a few sticks of dry manzanita, I reentered the burrow and kindled a fire from the previous night's coals. Before long I had coffee bubbling in a tin can.

Alonzo roused himself and sniffed. "Smells good." Then he noted the black oval of predawn sky framed in the doorway and muttered, "What time is it?"

"Five-thirty, near enough," I replied, tossing another handful of grounds into the boiling water. "You ready to go to work? Some folks are already getting after it."

Rolling himself up like a tumblebug, Alonzo

protested, "Too early. If you pan before full light, you're bound to lose some flakes. Call me at eight."

"Eight? It'll be sunup in less than an hour."

A snore that rattled the needles on the pine boughs over the door was the only response.

I spent the next couple of hours getting the lay of the land around Stringtown. Other folks there were friendly enough and willing to jawbone a bit when I carried the can of coffee around to share.

The mining method in use on the Feather River was based on the wing dam. A heap of stones, brush, wooden timbers, sandbags, or whatever was handy was built out into the creek, upstream of the claim. As this barrier shoved the current away from the shore, the area sheltered by the dam could be bailed out.

Once the water was mostly removed, the labor of digging down to bedrock began. Gold, being heavier than all the other minerals, naturally sank farthest until it could drop no further, being cuddled up next to solid rock. That was where the coarse flakes of the precious substance would be found.

Rousing Alonzo again, I thrust a cup of coffee into his hand and demanded that we go to the claim. "Burning daylight," I said. "Let's go get rich."

"Give me time to arrange my garb," he said with a grumpy sniff. He stood up, winced once and put his hand to his back, then shook all over like an old dog after a dirt bath. His clothes looked no different to me than they had when he was sleeping in them, but the adjustment must have suited him. "Let's go," he said. "I always do my best work before noon. Like the time up on the American River when I got up at five, found a five-pound nugget by seven and went back to bed."

We climbed over driftwood heaps, around gravel bars, past other miners working their claims, and finally followed a gully lined with heavy shale down to where it dead-ended at the stream's edge. "Here she is," Alonzo said majestically, waving his hand over a scene bare of any dam or digging. A shovel, an ax, and a pick lay on the ground.

"Where's the claim?" I demanded.

"Right there," Alonzo said, gesturing toward the tools. "Camp code says tools left at the site holds the claim."

"But where's the dam?"

"Ain't built yet."

"Timber? Sandbags? Boulders?"

"I told you, my partner up and died on me. I haven't had a chance to really get this going yet."

"Not really? It isn't going at all. What'd your partner die of, anyhow?"

"The indications here are real good," Alonzo said. "Go on, dig down at the bottom of the gully there and wash a pan."

There was no other way to learn prospecting than to do it. I dug down through the surface soil till I hit gravel and sand. Dumping a bladeful into a pan, I carried it to the stream.

"Catch a pint of water. That's it," Alonzo instructed. "Now, slosh it around in a circle. Easy! Just let the loose bits slop over the edge."

Several minutes passed of my plunging my hands into the chilly stream. Then Alonzo took over, gently washing the last fragments of sand. "Those black bits are iron," he said. "Heavy and tough to get shed of. But they are the sign that you're getting close. There, you see?"

Bending over the pan he held outstretched for my inspection, I squinted, but saw only black gravel. Noticing my frown, Alonzo moved so that the full light of the sun shown into the flat container. "Those two little yellow specks?"

"Chispa! Sparks in Spanish lingo. Sure sign we're on top of the pocket. Right out there." Alonzo waved toward the ripples of the river.

"So, what's the plan?" I queried. "Timbers backed by rocks and gravel over top?"

"Uh-huh," Alonzo agreed vaguely. "That's the ticket."

"There's a stand of alders on top of the draw that'll work," I said thoughtfully, "and we can dig manageable-size stones out of the shale face. Which do you want to do?"

Alonzo flinched and put his hand to his back. "I . . . I'd best sit in the sun some first. Let my spine warm up a mite. Old war wound, don't you see?"

"I thought it was your leg?" I said warily.

"Different war. Took a rifle ball down Mexico way," he explained. "Time Old Rough and Ready put me up for a medal. 'Twas at the Battle of Buena Vista . . ."

Without the dam in place there would be no getting down to the streambed where gold in any measurable quantity might be found. Without gold, all supplies, meager as they were, would be bought from Jameson on credit, to be paid off by future finds. It was a prison of sorts; hunting gold to get rich and then needing to find gold to get out of debt.

When my partner did no work at all the first day, was stricken with lumbago the second and quinsy the third, it was up to me to perform all the engineering. It crossed my mind somewhere between the lumbago and the quinsy to say good-bye to Mister Alonzo Root and take up my own claim.

The problems with that idea were these: The river was already claimed and staked for miles in both directions. Then too, searching the tributary canyons and ravines for a likely unclaimed spot could take weeks, and wet weather was closing in fast.

I chopped what seemed like a forest of quaking aspens, limbed them, and cut them into eight-foot lengths. When I had felled enough to replace our coyote den with a substantial log cabin, I carried them down to the stream.

A pair of boulders leaning against each other at the upstream boundary of the claim gave me a convenient starting point. I drove the sharpened spike of the first timber upright into the mud of the creekbed just where it could be braced by the rocks.

Next I rammed another as close to the first as possible, lashing the two together with strips of rawhide. (Purchased from Jameson on credit, of course.) I continued in this pattern, standing atop the boulders at first in order to hammer on the stakes with the butt of the ax. When the fence of timbers stretched too far out into the stream for me to reach the new additions, I added a walkway. This was formed by attaching crosspieces of tree trunks, wedged into place with whittled oak pegs.

Said I to my partner, "If you are unable to swing an ax or tote stones, do you suppose you could whittle pegs?"

This he allowed he could manage, and so sat beside the stream, carving wooden spikes and regaling me with stories of his exploits in Mexico, crossing the Plains, and wrestling grizzly bears in the Rockies.

"You heard of Carson? Kit Carson, the scout? Well, I saved his life once. Seems his rifle misfired, and just when a slavering grizzly was about to crush the life out of him, I jumped that bear from behind. Yes sir! Drove my bowie knife into his ribs."

To brace the pilings, I alternated days of extending the fence with hauling shale rock down from my quarry in the canyon. These I piled on my shoulders for want of a barrow or wagon and carried them to the claim. The dam came to take on solidity and thickness as I worked, until it was a substantial barricade, deflecting the water outward away from our bank.

Several days of bailing followed until the pool formed behind the dam was nothing but mud. That was when the real work commenced.

We panned the mud at the bottom of the swamped-out place and found enough color for Jameson to extend our credit to include a bucket. With this I hauled heavy clay sediment, sand, and gravel up to a pile on the beach.

When I picked up the bucket, I got something else as well. It was a letter from Elijah. He said he had located in

Marysville and was cooking for pay. I thought I'd try to look him up when the rising water drove us out of the hills.

Now that Alonzo had no further pegs to whittle, he occupied his time idly swirling pans full of gravel and exclaiming over this bit or that flake. "But nothing to compare with the nuggets that will soon be ours," he announced.

"Speaking of nuggets," I called from the six-foot-deep pit in which I was standing. Our dike was solid, but it was not waterproof, and I was up to my shins in cold ooze, despite the fact that every third bucket I hoisted was nothing but liquid. "Nuggets," I repeated. "When do I get to see those specimens?"

Alonzo looked alarmed. "Don't speak so loudly," he warned. "Do you want to wake up with your throat slit? What about all those miners that just up and disappear? You don't think I'd be fool enough to keep the gold near camp, do you? No sir! It's hid a good piece off in the woods."

"Why don't you fetch it down, then?"

I was ragging on him, of course. I had long since ceased to believe that there was any stash of nuggets; else why would the man live in a burrow and eat beans and salt pork?

"I'll fetch it in soon as it's safe. Say, did I ever tell you about the treasure room I run across in Chapultepec? General Winfield Scott . . ."

"I thought you were fighting with Zachary Taylor."

"That was later. This come first."

CHAPTER 13

On July 9, 1850, the president of the United States, Zachary Taylor, died of cholera. His vice president, Millard Fillmore, succeeded him.

It took two and a half months for news of that momentous event to come to California by ship via Panama or to stagger across the plains from Missouri. Jamie and the priest heard the report from a weary band of travelers in an immigrant train on their way to Marysville.

That same day the start of the great cholera plague hit a group of miners upriver. Eight men died within twenty-four hours of the first symptoms. Their deaths were thought to be caused by bad mule meat served at the shanty of Elijah, who had taken up his profession as cook in the gold camps. He and Scrimshaw were making thirty dollars in dust a day. Good wages.

Cholera put an end to his prosperity. The citizens of Marysville formed a mob and raided Elijah's cookshack. Scrimshaw took to the rafters and cussed them all as they dragged poor Elijah back to Marysville. They were near to lynching my old friend and would have done so if three dozen more fellows had not been struck with terrible stomach cramps and diarrhea in the midst of the trial. In the general dash for the bushes, someone had the realization that these new cases had not eaten at Elijah's shack. But such was the temper of the time that the crowd was looking for someone to blame, and Elijah was elected.

Jamie and the priest arrived in town. Spotting Elijah and asking for details, Jamie put the pieces together; she fought through the crowd and elbowed her way onto the back of the hayrick where Elijah stood bound with a rope around his neck. Startled by the fortitude and determination and the womanliness of Jamie, the mob fell silent.

"Mizz Jamie!" cried Elijah. "They think I pizzened some gentlemen up the river a piece."

"They mean to hang you, Elijah," she said sternly. Spreading her arms she cried in a loud voice, "Citizens of Marysville. I am here to offer you momentous news from the East! President Taylor is dead of the cholera." She paused long enough for the rumble of sorrow and astonishment to ripple through the crowd. Then she continued. "Yes. President Taylor is dead these eleven weeks past. And the very disease that killed the president of the United States is no respecter of persons!" Here she hesitated for a long, dramatic moment. "And I tell you that the same plague is here to carry you away as well!"

A long and terrible groan issued from the men. "What do you know about it?" called an unbeliever from the back of the crowd. "The old fool poisoned those fellows and we'll have him hanged for it."

Defiantly Jamie removed the rope from around

Elijah's neck. Father Patrick, red-faced and panting, climbed to join her. He positioned himself in front of Elijah lest some member of the jury finish the trial with a bullet in Elijah's head.

Father Patrick raised his fist and challenged, "Will you die with the blood of an innocent man on your hands? What the widow O'Reilly says to you about the cholera is true! It's only a matter of time before the plague takes hold among you all. Get to your own camps and tend to your own souls. Death will be calling on you soon enough."

From the mouth of the priest, the fate of hundreds was pronounced. What had begun in the East had finally overtaken the West. Ships of the eastern seaboard carried passengers infected with the disease to New Orleans. From there they traveled upriver to St. Louis. Cholera spread like wildfire through the Missouri outfitting towns and from there it moved across the Plains with the immigrants. On the wagon trains children were orphaned. The wife who buried her husband one day might be dead herself the next. The trail to California was inscribed plain by the crude markers above shallow graves.

Jamie had seen the ravages of cholera before. She was among those who survived the Dublin outbreak of 1845. Two sisters and a brother had perished in that year. Jamie, however, was left with an immunity and a rage against the sickness, making her the ideal nurse for those in Marysville who fell ill within the next week.

Elijah was immune as well. Whether he had endured the sickness in his younger days or was simply strong against it I cannot say. He worked along beside her in those terrible days. A canvas lean-to became the hospital. The clearing at the base of the large water oak at the edge of the encampment became morgue, and the field beyond it, cemetery.

Scrimshaw, brought from the cookshack to perch on a ladder-back chair, looked upon the human parade of misery without much comment. Then from the prayers of the priest and the sufferers, the bird learned to say, "Bless me!" and "Amen!"

This made an odd dialogue when a miner brought his dying partner to the tent.

"Ma'am, my friend is fallen ill."

"Amen!" Scrimshaw cried.

"He asked I bring him here before he passed in his chips."

"Bless me! Bless me! Bless me!" the bird interjected.

"I fear he's gravely ill," said Jamie. "His brow has the dew of death upon it."

Scrimshaw agreed. "Aye-aye, Cap'n. Amen! Bless me!"

The bird made a correct diagnosis in that case. The patient was dead within the hour. Jamie could tell from a look at the wrinkled skin and ashen cast of the complexion who was past hope.

A mass grave was dug for those who came too late to seek her help. But she saved fully half of those who reached her in time. Dosing the patients heavily with laudanum, her treatment drugged them to a state of insensibility and halted both flux and vomiting, saving the inner fluids. The priest wondered if such heavy doses of the narcotic would not finish off what the cholera began, but it was the only specific known.

In this matter Jamie warned him to stick to his specialty. "No doubt you will have enough customers to pray over and bury. As to the cholera, I learned the treatment from my own experience. Those whom the laudanum saves will thank me. Those who die in spite of it shall be grateful they were unconscious."

The priest said no more until one week into the ordeal he came to her shaking and ashen. "You and Elijah shall have double duty now, girl. I fear I have need of a dose of laudanum." At this, Father Patrick collapsed.

With Elijah's help Jamie laid the priest out in the coolest corner of the canvas hospital. She cleaned him and sponged him until he opened his eyes. Grasping her hand, he whispered, "If I leave this earth, you must take Danny's confession to San Jose. To the authorities."

"Don't speak now, Father. You'll take it to them yourself and that's a promise."

Elijah cradled the priest's head in his arms. Jamie filled the spoon with a mixture of laudanum, acetate of lead, and bismuth and ladled it into his mouth, offering this benediction with the medicine, "Sweet dreams to you, Father. We shall meet on the other side of sleep."

He sputtered and swallowed the bitter draught, then squeezed her hand. "I fear I shall not awaken. Promise . . . Danny's letter. It tells full thirty men who died at the hands of a foul gang. . . . Promise me you will take . . ."

"I promise. I promise we will take it together. Now let sleep hold you for a while, and when you awaken we'll speak more on the matter."

The priest slipped quickly into the deep slumber of the drug.

Elijah's worried gaze locked on Jamie's face. He looked past her to where a grim-faced patient was staring hard at her. Elijah said in a hushed tone, "That fella Clyde Wick is mighty int'rested in what the padre said."

Turning slightly, she observed the dark eyes of the man. He studied her with a hostile glare; this in spite of the fact she had saved his life.

"Widow O'Reilly," Clyde Wick questioned. "It's said you're the widow of Robert Daniels. Is it so?"

She replied with a nod. "I am, though out here he called himself by a name other than the one I held in tender regard. His true name was Danny."

Clyde grunted. "Don't matter what name he went by. I worked with him, freighting for Marrasco. Mebbe he wrote you about me?"

"No, he did not," she remarked, rising from her place beside Father Patrick.

There was no gratitude in Wick's voice when he muttered, "Strange that his widder would be the one nursin' me back to health. Right strange."

There was something foreboding in his look and the tone of his voice. Jamie instructed Elijah to move Clyde Wick out of the tent and onto a pallet outside beside the riverbank where the recovering men were cared for.

Come morning, the scoundrel was gone without any word of thanks or recognition that Jamie had saved his wretched life. Clyde Wick carried with him the nagging suspicion that Danny O'Reilly had not gone silent to his grave.

At ten feet down I finally hit a gravel bed. This, Alonzo told me, was the proof positive that we were almost to solid rock against which all the wealth of the Sierras would be nestling. "We'll pan all this gravel as we go," he said. I noted with some skepticism the plural personal pronoun, but let it pass. "When we've cleared it up, we'll be digging out chunks of solid gold."

My morning began by climbing down a makeshift ladder into the three feet of water that had accumulated overnight and bailing out the dig. I had rigged an A-frame boom with a counterweight to aid me in lifting buckets out of the deep crevasse. My machinery relieved some of the exertion, but did nothing to speed the process. Each time I filled a bucket I had to climb up the ladder, dump the refuse, and then lower the pail and myself down again.

I did enlist Alonzo in operating a cradle. This was a wooden contraption like an orange crate with a spout and a handle. I shoveled in a load of pay dirt, added a couple buckets of water, and then left Alonzo to rock the device down to gold and heavier elements.

For once he had actually been telling a half-truth. There was gold in the gravel; not much, but enough to collect in a little jar. The first day we eked out an ounce, or about sixteen dollars' worth. On a practical level it meant making enough of a payment to Jameson to refill an empty flour sack and collect two tins of sardines.

The oily fish made me miss Scrimshaw. I wondered

how he was faring. I knew that Elijah was taking good care of him, but I wondered if in his feathered brain he missed me some way. Of course, thinking about Scrimshaw also made me think about Jamie O'Reilly; a thought that I put aside as quickly as I could.

The second day we cleaned up thirty-two dollars' worth. The flakes were indeed coarse, like heavy parchment torn into tiny scraps. I took back half of the evil things I had been thinking about Alonzo.

The third morning was dark well past my usual hour of rising. The sky was black with clouds and there was a chilly wind blowing up the river. I worked in the pit anyway, casting a couple of anxious thoughts toward the quality of my construction. I did not want to be fifteen feet below water level in a narrow, confined space should the dam suddenly break. Odd how that worry never came to me when the sun was shining. It had never crossed my mind before.

In between my seventh and eighth bucket loads, I heard Alonzo talking to someone. When I popped out the top of the ladder I saw that it was a trio of miners. They had packs on their backs, heavily loaded by the looks of them. From the line of their march, they were headed downstream.

"Yep, we're through for the winter," their leader supplied. "River's already rising and what with the rain a-comin', it's time to skedaddle till next spring."

"Not us," my partner vowed with a hasty glance in my direction. "Plenty of time still. Rising water could wipe out all our hard work. Can't afford to quit now."

The three miners shrugged, felt the thin patter of

raindrops with their outstretched hands, and trudged off westward. "Pay them no mind," Alonzo urged. "Their type is just afraid of hard work, that's all."

I was grateful he had no anecdote to illustrate that point. I might have felt compelled to smack him in the nose.

By the end of the day I had reached the solid rock underlying the gravel of the ancient streambed. There were no chunks of gold waiting to be carried up like thousand-dollar bricks. Worse, the rocks of the river's floor were flat, large, and pressed tightly together. There were no likely crevices in which real gold nuggets, however small, might be hiding.

I exploded up out of the ditch. "You filthy liar!" I screamed at Alonzo. "There's naught but paving stones down there!" I felt flushed and feverish in my temper; rage I did not often permit myself and it made me feel peculiar.

"Now, now," Alonzo soothed. "It's a good sign. We'll shift the stones tomorrow. Think of all the gold . . ."

"Shift the stone!" I shouted. "Are you crazy? It'll take ten men with block and tackle all day to shift one!"

It was raining harder now and almost too dark to see. "Let's knock off," Alonzo offered. "We've got most a hundred dollars washed out. What say we get some more sardines and celebrate?"

"You celebrate," I growled, my gorge rising at just the thought of the canned fish. "I feel punk. I'm going to bed."

CHAPTER 14

I was trapped in the bottom of the shaft and the dam was about to burst. I struggled with the ladder, but there was a rope tangled around my legs. The wall of boulders and timbers bulged ominously, ready at any second to give way.

Yelling for help, I called for Elijah to save me. No, that was not possible, he was nowhere around. Nuck Gutterson. That was it! Nuck would save me.

The water was rising to the level of my chest. Raising my eyes to the bit of sunlight at the top of the passage, I called again for help. Nuck's face appeared at the rim of the well. He spoke no word, only shook his head sadly and disappeared. "Nuck!" I yelled. "I saved your life! Help me!" Then I remembered: That was not possible either. Nuck was dead, killed in the explosion on the ship.

The water rose to my chin. I felt the dam pressing against my back, pushing me into the ladder, then crushing me against the other wall of the dig. I was being squeezed and drowned at the same time.

"Help!" I thrashed. "God, help me!"

Someone grasped my shoulder, shook it, called my name. An angel? "Jamie?"

There was an explosive curse and my face, which had broken the surface of the water, was shoved back down. Not an angel then; a murderer.

"I know what this is," a voice muttered. "I seen this before. Rafer, I'll go get help." From a great distance I heard Alonzo's voice. "I'll be back."

I mumbled something, pleaded with him not to desert me. What was real? Where was I? The ropes entangling my feet dissolved into a blanket wrapped and twisted around me. The shaft of the mine turned into the walls of our burrow. "Don't leave me," I begged.

The pressure was still there, building, expanding, readying to burst me apart. *What?* My mind screamed. *What is it? Has the cavern collapsed?*

Hot and cold at the same time, I felt someone roughly rolling me over, riffling my pockets. "Goodbye," Alonzo's voice said.

I raised my head. Gray light was coming into the cave. I saw Alonzo's back as he left me. I crawled toward the entrance, my legs unable to bear my weight.

The pressure built to an excruciating agony. Then a gasp was torn from me as my innards exploded with a bloody flux. I fell backward into the shaft and the waters closed over my head.

I was swimming up from the bottom of a well. My lungs did not hurt and I was not panicked for air, and yet my movements were slow, sluggish. There was a small circle of light toward which I was moving. I wondered if I was still in the Stringtown burrow, still crawling toward the cave entrance.

A voice called my name. "Rafer," it whispered from far away. "Rafer, can you hear me?" It had a sweet inflection, calming; not Alonzo then. Who? "Rafer, wake up and drink a bit of this."

Strong arms raised me under my shoulders and a deeper voice than the other rumbled close to the back of my head. "You sho he's gonna make it?" It sounded like Elijah, but could not be. How could Elijah find me in Stringtown?

"Help me here, Elijah," the softer inflection was in front of me. "He needs to swallow a drop of this beef broth."

"Yes, Mizz Jamie."

Jamie! My vision, which had been wandering around the narrow tunnel through which I was passing, snapped into focus. There, not six inches from my own face and printed with deep concern, were the features of Jamie O'Reilly. "Jamie," I managed to mumble. "How? Where?"

"Hush now, Rafer," she soothed, "take a sip." A wooden spoon pressed into my mouth. I lapped, tentatively at first, at the warm, fragrant broth. Then, more greedily, I slurped it down. She giggled, a nervous laugh of relief. "See, 'Lijah," she exclaimed. "I told you he'd make it now."

"But how did you . . ." My innards were quieted, but not my mind. Where was I, and how did these angels of mercy find me?

"Hush," Jamie insisted, ladling more soup into me, and then giving me a sip of water. "Don't fuss yourself now. Sleep more and we'll talk after."

Though I wanted to know more right then, my consciousness betrayed me. Unutterable weariness closed over my head, and I sank back down into dense, deep waters.

When I next woke, it was dark, but this darkness was real and not just part of my illness. A fire crackled outside the tent where I lay on a cot. Through the flap that was partly folded back, I could see someone stirring a stewpot over the cookfire. When the figure turned sideways, I could make out her dear profile. "Jamie," I called, intending to sound her name in manly tones. Instead it came out a feeble croak. "Jamie," I repeated. "Missus O'Reilly."

A squawk much like my own noise erupted near my bed. Twisting my head around, I saw Scrimshaw perched on a wooden limb stuck in the ground beside me. When I looked at him, he ducked his head five times in rapid succession and gave another loud screech of joy.

Jamie O'Reilly entered the tent at that. "He's been so worried about you," she said. "Kept watch over you day and night."

"And he was not the only watcher, I think."

Blushing, Jamie looked down at the dirt floor, then up at the guy rope, then finally back at me. "How are you feeling, Captain Maddox?"

"It was Rafer when I was still drifting," I scolded.

She colored even deeper and stuttered a little in trying to hide her embarrassment. "Will you have more soup then? It will help you get your strength back the quicker."

My stomach growled its agreement, but I fended off its insistent complaint. "First, I'd like a few answers," I said. "Where am I, and how did I get here?" I studied her face, wishing I could get her to look in my eyes. Where was her husband? Why did he not take her out of this place of misery and sickness? But how glad I was he had not!

"You're in Marysville," she said. "As to the how, you can thank your friend Alonzo."

"Alonzo," I snorted. "He robbed me and left me for dead." Then it struck me that she had never met Alonzo to my knowledge. How did she know his name?

"You wrong him," she corrected. "He found the note from Elijah in your jacket." I remembered Alonzo fumbling through my clothing. "He gathered some men and made them help carry you all the way down from String-town in the rain. Two of them took sick on the way. One died. But Alonzo got you here inside a day. Any later and the laudanum would not have saved you."

"But you," I pondered. "How do you come to be here?"

"I'm helping a priest, Father Patrick," she said briefly. "Together we have been tending the sick, except that the good father was also stricken. Saints be praised, he is recovering. Now, enough of this catechism. Drink more soup and get your strength." There was much more I wanted to know, but I did as she instructed.

Later, Elijah came to see me. He explained about

Jamie's murdered husband and how Jamie and Father Patrick had saved 'Lijah's neck from the mob. "And where is Alonzo?" I asked. "I need to thank him and apologize for thinking evil of him."

The cook's face split into a grin. "He's long gone, scared stiff 'bout this cholera. Mizz Jamie explained he prob'ly could not take it now, what with his partner dying of it and him being so near it an' all."

"I'm his partner," I corrected, confused.

"Naw. His other partner, befo' you." That explained a lot. "Anyways," Elijah continued, "he says the claim is all yours, if you lives. He says he's heard of a beach where the sand is all gold dust and he lit a shuck for there."

My gaze swept past the shoulder of my friend to follow Jamie as she moved from cot to cot offering encouragement to my fellow patients.

Elijah grinned. "You was callin' her name the whole time."

Taking account of my hard luck and impoverishment I replied, "She'll get swept away by some fella who's struck it rich."

"She paid particular mind to you, Rafer. You shoulda been dead by my reckonin', if she hadn't made such a fuss over you." He paused and said in a half-whisper. "She be needin' a good man now."

Did I dare allow myself to hope that I could be the man for Jamie? I closed my eyes and drifted off to sleep only to dream of her against my will.

I opened my eyes in the soft light of predawn. Jamie hovered over me. Her soft, cool fingers stroked my forehead.

"Are you real?" I asked.

She smiled. "You were calling my name."

I hoped I had not said more, for the vision I had of her in my unconscious state was not something I wanted known to her in my waking hours.

Stammering, I replied, "I am sorry to hear about your husband." This was not the truth. I was glad she was free.

Jamie considered my statement. There was amusement in her eyes. "Are you?"

"He was a fool to leave you behind."

"The road he traveled I could not have walked. I suspected he had gone wrong. Now I am sure of it. I still do not know everything, but I am certain he was involved in something terrible. It cost him everything. I grieve only for what he once was."

I blurted the question that had been troubling me since I watched her walk away in San Francisco. "Why did you leave me . . . the ship . . . when we arrived?"

She was quiet for a time, considering how best to answer. "Because . . . because you had invaded my dreams, Rafer, and I was defenseless." She leaned down and kissed my forehead. "Now it seems I have entered yours as well."

It was my turn to blush. "I cannot deny it." Grasping her hand I pulled her closer to me.

"What will we do about it?"

"When I can stand up before the priest . . ."

"And when he can stand as well?" She searched my face with such tender longing that I knew our waking hours together would be even sweeter than the dreams had been.

CHAPTER 15

I was fifteen days getting my strength back. The padre and I shared the tent and our healing progressed along the same lines. The cholera has two phases: The first, acute stage causes death within forty-eight hours if the flux is not reduced. If a man survives that period, the odds are good that he will make a complete recovery, provided he takes no new ill and has somebody to see to his feed.

Of course, we had the best care possible. Jamie spooned beef tea mixed with tincture of iron into Father Patrick and me for a week solid. And speaking of iron, she ruled our days with an iron fist, ordering us to eat and commanding us when to lie back on the cots. The priest and I were both so weak that we did not even argue, much.

Meanwhile the plague had run its course. Reports were slow coming in from the upper mines, but the count appeared to be fifty-two dead. Were it not for Alonzo and Jamie, I would have made the fifty-third. It was very sobering to think about.

During my time of recuperation, I was still suffering nightmares of drowning or of being abandoned in the Stringtown burrow. Many nights I woke in a cold sweat, fussing and thrashing, with Father Patrick trying to comfort me and rattling his beads with a mighty host of prayers.

So it did not surprise me much to dream of someone going through my belongings. This was different than usual, because I could see the figure clearly, not dim and foggy as the visions had been. Then too, I felt only curiosity, not the consuming dread that had attacked my nights.

As I studied this form tossing my clothing about, he turned away and began riffling Father Patrick's belongings. That was when it struck me: If I could see the tent and recognize the priest, then this was not a dream!

I hollered 'help!' and 'stop thief' as loud as I could and the man disappeared. Father Patrick jumped with a start, praying for my spirit to quiet down. It took me a time to convince him that the apparition had been real. When he saw the disordered state of his cassock, which had been folded at the foot of the cot, he believed me.

Nothing appeared to have been taken, but Father Patrick thought he knew the cause of the nocturnal attack just the same. "Stay here whilst I fetch Jamie," he said. He did not tell me then, but the reason for rousing her was to see that she was all right. She was lodging in a small frame house nearby and came at once, a gray wool shawl over her long cotton nightgown.

We three sat in council together. "The burglar was

after Danny's confession," explained Father Patrick. "The killers are afraid of being found out. Tell me, Rafer, what did this man look like?"

"Lean and ill-favored," I said at once. "Dark hair and a scar below one eye."

"Clyde Wick!" Jamie said with a clap of her hands. "He has come back."

"What's this all about, Father?" I asked. "Is Jamie in danger?"

Father Patrick shook his head. "I cannot say more just now," he said.

"But I think I know the man, Wick. Let me tell you my surmise. If you just confirm or deny my guesses, will that violate anything?"

"No," the priest agreed, warming to the idea. "Begin, my boy."

"Danny's confession identifies miners who have disappeared on the river."

"It does," the father confirmed.

"And Danny was employed by those whom he thinks were involved."

"True again."

"And his letter names or at least suggests Marrasco."

"Well done," Father Patrick praised. "You have it all correct."

"But how comes Wick to be here?" I wondered. "Marrasco operates between Sacramento and the bay."

Here Jamie put in her oar. "Not these four weeks past," she said. "He and Wakeman have come to an agreement to rule the river between them. *New World* sails between Sac City and Frisco and *Goliath* runs the upper river. I saw her at the wharf below here today."

Here was news indeed. My old mentor and my old enemy had joined forces. What an evil conspiracy they made together. Much was already explained by what we now knew: Marrasco's night passages and the string of vanishing prospectors were connected.

"Your husband was killed for trying to report what he knew?" I asked Jamie. I saw a look pass between the priest and woman.

Father Patrick, to change the subject, said, "I think we must talk about . . ."

"No, Father," Jamie corrected. "Rafer is a good man and shall hear the truth." Then to me she said, "Danny was involved in the plot. He lured men to their deaths. But one man's killing, another Irishman, went especially hard with him. He got no sleep after that . . ."

"The fenced plot on the river!" I said. "Danny is the one who tended the grave."

Jamie nodded, weeping softly. "His remorse was too great and he wanted out of the band, but they feared he would tell, so they killed him. It must have been Wick who did it!"

"But why haven't you told anyone before this? To save the lives of others is a higher calling than even a man's dying confession!"

"Tush, my boy! It's not that," the priest said, relieved to be able to unburden. "Danny wrote to trust no one except a U.S. marshal or the army. He said the mayor and the local constables were all getting part of the swag not to ask too many questions."

Jamie's eyes flashed fire and her back was ramrod straight. How I loved the steel in that girl! "So what do we do now?" she said, with anger in her words. "How many more will die before they are stopped?"

"I am well enough to make the journey to San Jose," Father Patrick vowed. "I'll start tomorrow."

The best plans, it seems, do not always work out. Before Father Patrick had finished naming San Jose, the tent flap was swept aside and in burst Walter Buck and Clyde Wick. Both were armed, with five-shooters at the ready; there was no doubt that they meant business.

"Pity you all are too smart for your own good," Buck intoned without smiling. "Now that you've tumbled to the scheme, you'll get to see firsthand how right you were!"

"Let the girl go," Father Patrick demanded. "You cannot mean to hurt a woman. Stop and think, man! No place will ever be safe to you hereafter and every hand will be against you if you offer her any harm."

I thought that his words shook Wick a mite, but not Walter Buck. "Who's ever gonna know?" he sneered. "After we drop you in the river?"

"But what about the colored feller?" Wick blurted in a panicky-sounding voice. "Don't forget him."

"Been thinking on that," Buck said with a nonchalance of evil. "It don't matter that he ain't here. Fact is, it works out better this way. We'll pin the blame on him for the killings. Then he'll get lynched for certain. Shoot, there might even be a reward for catching him!" Buck snickered at his own wit.

They marched us out of the tent, and down toward the river landing. As we drew nearer I could see the orange fire glowing in the smokestack. It was an evil sight, that sinister gleam in the dark. The faint puff of steam and smoke showed that *Goliath* was ready to sail.

Marrasco, devil's spawn that he was, met us at the gangplank. "Got them all?" he asked. "Any trouble?"

"Not a bit," Buck asserted. "It was just like you figered. We took them all together, except for the colored man." Then he explained his plan regarding Elijah.

"That's good." Marrasco chuckled, the point of his spade beard wagging up and down. "Take them all below to the engine room. There's just the three of us aboard tonight, so no chance of any witnesses. Wick, you stand guard and Buck, you be ready to cast off. We'll bring them up one at a time after we reach Horseshoe Bend. There's a nice deep pool there to sink them in."

We were herded belowdecks into *Goliath*'s boiler room. Once there, Wick lined us up opposite the gangway and covered us with his pistol. Almost at once the bell rang for slow ahead, and Buck returned from untying the lines. "Come on, Walter," Wick said. "Give me a hand with the bar."

"Use your head," Buck snorted. "The old priest and the girl are no danger, but I don't like the look in this other feller's eye. I'll cover them; you use the bar and be quick about it."

"Why'nt you tie them up?"

"Just get on with it!" Buck snapped, waving the revolver around as he left Wick to do all the work of setting the steamer in motion.

"You'll never get away with this," I suggested.

"Shut up," Buck demanded, "or I'll just shoot you and toss you over right here." Then as soon as Marrasco had signaled for ahead full, Walter Buck left Wick to watch us while he went up to confer with Marrasco in the pilothouse.

Wick made us sit on the floor with our backs to him, while he squatted on the lowest step of the gangway. "Mister Wick," Father Patrick said in a cajoling voice. "I know that at heart you are no killer. Especially I know you would not drop the hammer on she who saved your life."

"Leave off!" Wick said. "There's nothing I can do about it! If I don't help them they'd kill me!"

"Like what happened to Danny O'Reilly?" I asked. "How big a mistake can you make and not wind up six feet under?"

"Shut up!"

"Did you kill Missus O'Reilly's husband?" Father Patrick asked. "And then received mercy at her hands?"

"It wasn't me!" Wick fairly shouted. "It was Buck who done it!"

"We could help you escape their clutches," Father Patrick promised. "Help you go to the authorities."

"Stop talking!" Wick said, and he flung a chunk of stove wood at the priest.

The wedge of timber struck Father Patrick a glancing

blow to the head, but knocked him to the floor just the same. A thin trickle of blood creased the father's cheek, and Jamie tore a strip from the hem of her nightgown to staunch the wound. "How could you?" she demanded. "You are no man. You are a worm."

"Just keep still!" Wick cried again. "I told you to keep shut!"

He was near breaking. Wick's nervous debility might have worked to our advantage, giving me the chance to overpower him, or his jitters might have made him shoot us all and have done. In the end, it was neither.

There came a scratching at the hatch, like fingernails on a desktop. "What's that?" Wick asked the air. Prudently, Jamie and I kept silent. She tended the still-unconscious priest.

The sound came again. "Maybe it's the ghost of another victim," I said softly.

"You don't move!" Wick screeched. "Don't even wiggle!" The scraping sound came again from the hatchway. Wick, pistol trembling violently in his hand, went to the top of the stairs. "Who's there?"

There was no reply but the same rasp of claws. "The devil come to claim his own," I muttered softly over my shoulder.

Wick spun around on the landing like a top, waving the pistol in looping arcs. "Shut up! Shut up!" Then to the door he said, "Who's there? Answer or I'll shoot through the panel!" There was no response; in fact, the scratching ceased.

Wick stood there uncertainly for a moment, then

thrusting the pistol forward like a talisman to ward off evil, he undogged the hatch and opened it.

There at his feet flapped Scrimshaw. The bird fluttered past him before Wick could stoop, flapped down the steps and came to me. "What the . . ." Our jailer was facing us again, but he had not shut the hatch.

From out of the night at either side of the doorway shot a pair of arms. Those on the right were Elijah's. They grasped Wick's gunhand, beat his wrist against the metal railing, sending the pistol flying. The other hands belonged to Danny O'Reilly's tongueless friend, the man called Gabby.

Together Elijah and Gabby flung Wick headfirst down the steps. His head collided with the crank of the steam valve and down he went.

Grabbing the gun, I posted myself at the head of the steps in case Walter Buck should return. Since there was no sign that anyone had heard the ruckus I asked, "'Lijah, how'd you find us? And why'd you bring Scrimshaw?"

"Easy," he said. "I was awake and seen the light at your place. I was listenin' when Buck give his speech. I rounded up Gabby and we come after. Scrimshaw just come of his own accord."

"Shall we stop the boat?" Jamie wanted to know.

"No," I said. "That would tip off Marrasco that something was up."

Gabby pointed at Wick, who was stirring on the metal grate of the deck. The mute man pantomimed tying Wick up.

"Got no rope." Elijah observed. "Does we leave the pistol with Jamie or does one of us three stay to guard Wick?"

"Neither," I said, scooting back down to kneel beside the groggy Wick. Patting his face, I pulled him upright and leaned him back in the corner below the steam pressure gauge. Snapping my fingers, I called Scrimshaw to me, then set the bird on Wick's left shoulder. "Wick," I said, slapping him harder. "Wick, pay attention."

His unfocused eyes opened and he blinked. "What?"

"This parrot on your shoulder is vicious," I said. "Do you see this?" I fingered the notch Scrimshaw had taken out of my ear. "He's bloodthirsty, Wick! If you move without Mizz O'Reilly's say-so, he's gonna peck your eyes out. Do you understand?"

I plucked Scrimshaw's tail feathers. He struck at my hand and growled at me; a savage sound, uttered deep in the bird's throat. "I understand!" Wick pleaded. "Don't let him hurt me!"

To Jamie I handed the Johnson bar and whispered, "When he's more awake he may be less scared. If he shows any fight at all, lambast him with this."

"I can and I will," she vowed. "Just look what he's done to poor Father Patrick!"

I circled the port side of the main deck while Elijah and Gabby went the starboard. We had not traveled more than half the length forward to the pilothouse when over the rush of the paddle wheels and the sighing of the steam engine came the ringing of the signal bell. It was Marrasco, calling for a stop. We had arrived at the place of intended execution. That it was to have been my place of execution was not lost on me.

A few moments of continued chuffing downstream and the bell rang again, insistently this time. Marrasco was impatient for his commands to be obeyed. I knew what would happen next. He would send Walter Buck down to see what was wrong. Since I was the one carrying the pistol, I hoped Buck would come my way. Elijah and Gabby were unarmed.

Creeping as quietly as I could, I reached the bottom of the ladder outside the salon. The pilothouse was one deck above me and just forward of where I stood.

A shot rang out on the far side of the ship and I heard a cry of pain. There was no time to lose. Whatever the outcome of the other combat, it was now up to me to disarm Marrasco.

I swarmed up the steps, rushing toward the wheelhouse hatch. Just before reaching it, I stopped and kicked it open, ducking back out of the way. I do not know why I thought to do that, since an instant before all my plans were bent on haste. It is too miraculous to call luck or instinct: divine Providence saved me.

As the hatch flew open, the blast of a shotgun tore the top half of the panel away, blowing the fragments over the rail and into the river. One barrel or two?

Then I heard the unmistakable sounds of someone fumbling with shot and powder; reloading. I sprinted around the corner, confronting Marrasco beside the helm station.

Another man would have reversed the single barrel

twelve gauge and used it as a club, but not he. Marrasco flung the weapon aside and flicked a knife from his shirt collar with his left hand.

All this I saw by the thin glow of the shielded chart table lamp. Otherwise the pilothouse was in total darkness. "I've been waiting for this chance," he said, advancing toward me.

"Hold it," I ordered. "I've got a gun." I pointed Wick's five-shooter at Marrasco's chest.

We formed a frozen tableau, Marrasco's face a mask of hatred, for all of five seconds. Then *Goliath*, which had been steaming downriver at top speed for several minutes longer than planned, climbed a sandbar. The starboard paddle wheel ramped upward sharply, throwing me backward through the pilothouse hatch. My hand struck the railing and the pistol flipped over my head to land with a splash far below.

Even before the revolver hit the water, Marrasco was on me. The impact with the shoal flung him after me, his knife slashing with murderous intent.

I caught his left arm as it swept toward my ribs. I tried to even the contest by smashing his wrist on the rail, but he jerked his knife hand upward and the blade ripped into my forearm. I backed away suddenly, rounding the pilothouse front. The pain, the loss of blood, and my recent illness combined to make the deck swirl under me.

Goliath continued to rattle along the west bank of the river. It rolled over tule reeds and willow thickets. It tried to climb a cottonwood before settling back. Then it hit another sandbar, plunging and bucking like the rankest mustang.

Marrasco slashed at me again, his face showing delight mixed with rage. When he lunged I caught the wrist of the knife hand with both of mine, trapping the weapon against the glass. It was all I could do to hang on.

A flicker of doubt flashed in my head. Why was Marrasco not using his other hand in the struggle for the blade? Then I saw the answer: He dropped his right hand to his waistband and drew another dagger.

Once again I jerked out of the way, but this time I did not relinquish my grip on his arm.

Goliath caromed off a boulder, shattering her starboard wheel and sending the ship into a vicious skid to the right. That motion, combined with my sudden lurch back, threw Marrasco off balance. Already overstretched in his eagerness to finish me, his midsection came under my shoulder and I flipped him up.

Over the railing he sailed, screaming. He bounced off the main deck awning. Marrasco flung out his hand to save himself, but because both fists were still holding knives, he could not catch ahold. Over the side he went, just ahead of the thrashing portside wheel.

I saw his dark head bob up once, just before the paddle wheel rode over the top of him, grinding him into the mud. *Goliath* gave a scream like a jungle beast whose bloodlust had been satisfied, and then shuddered to a stop.

There was still Walter Buck to deal with. Who had

been in front of the pistol shot I had heard? Where was Buck now, and was Jamie safe?

Racing sternward again, I collided headlong with someone. I threw a hard left, then a solid right that hurt my wounded arm before Elijah grabbed me around the middle and said, "Easy, Rafer. It's me."

"Jamie?" I panted. "Missus O'Reilly?"

"She's fine," he said. "Got mussed a little by the crashin' in the brush, but not as mussed as Wick."

"How come?"

"She thumped him 'longside the head with that Johnson bar," he reported. "Gabby is back with 'em now, so they're alright."

"And Buck? I heard a shot."

"I know . . . we was rasslin' for the gun when it went off . . . kilt him, Rafer. Marrasco?"

I shook my head. "He went under a paddle wheel."

"Then I reckon that's the end."

Dawn was just breaking over the Sierra as I tied a bandanna around my arm. The light trickling down the canyons illuminated the river in a pale gray glow. Just ahead of where the steamer had stopped was a massive oak tree. Had we run up on it, the boat would have been turned into kindling, and us along with it. "Is *Goliath*'s boiler going to blow?"

"I should say not!" Elijah retorted. "You ain't the only one what knows about relief valves!"

EPILOGUE

Clyde Wick ratted out the rest of the gang. Shortly thereafter, the new California attorney general, pushed along by the *Independent* and the *Alta Californian*, and backed by Governor Burnett, cleaned house. Though the flood of immigration into the Golden State was still on, a sudden urge to see Oregon struck Mayor North and several of his cronies.

Shortly after the river pirates were cleared away, I went to piloting again. *New World*'s builder, William Brown, came west, having finally won his legal battle with Sidney Jackson. Brown fired Wakeman for his misdeeds, then offered me my old job back.

I was pleased to be able to tell him no. A consortium of merchants, headed by undertaker Kleinman and advised by Leidesdorf and Squires, decided to enter the steamship business with a boat of their own. Brand-spanking new, *Queen City* was the fastest and the plushest boat on the river; and she was mine.

Even better was the fact that she plied her trade between Marysville and Sacramento City, because I made my residence in Marysville and I slept home nights. This was not only important to me, but my wife thought it a good provision too: Jamie and I married a year to the day after pulling me through the cholera. Father Patrick officiated, Elijah gave the bride away, and Scrimshaw shouted, "Amen!" Of course, he also added, "Sardines! Sardines! Hello! Hello! Hello!"

GEOGRAPHICAL NOTE

The delta of California is a thousand square miles of waterways and swamplands, willow thickets and cottonwood groves. All the snowmelt from the northern peaks clear to Mount Shasta, and all the rainfall on southern stretches all the way to the Tehachapis drains toward the delta.

The mighty rivers of California—the American, the Mokelumne, the San Joaquin, and the Sacramento—converge in the delta, flowing into San Francisco Bay before joining the deeps of the Pacific Ocean. If all the sloughs, byways, creeks, and channels were straightened out and laid end to end, they would stretch clear across the continent and partway back.

In 1846, the Bear Flag Rebellion wrested California from Mexico. In the minds of many it was not worth fighting over; too remote, too wild, too dangerous, too without promise.

Then in 1848, the peace of the region was shattered with the discovery of gold at Sutter's Mill, near the town of Coloma, just east of the delta. Almost overnight the character of the area changed as hundreds and then thousands of gold seekers flooded in from the States and foreign countries.

Gold changed California from a sleepy, backwater territory into the object of the greatest spontaneous migration in the history of the world. Overnight, gold created a new society out of men who had nothing in common except pans, shovels, and the desire to be rich.

Gold changed California, but it did not change the delta. Even though flood control dams and irrigation projects have siphoned off much of the water that once flowed through the district, it is still full of intrigue, history, and adventure.